SONIA ALLISON'S FOOD PROCESSOR COOKBOOK

SONIA ALLISON'S FOOD PROCESSOR COOKBOOK

Written with
Patricia Hudson

PIATKUS

© 1980 Sonia Allison and Patricia Hudson
First published in Great Britain in 1980 by
Judy Piatkus (Publishers) Limited of Loughton, Essex

ISBN 0 86188 064 1

Allison, Sonia
    Sonia Allison's food processor cookbook.
    I. Food processor cookery
    I. Hudson, Patricia
    II. Food processor cookbook
    641.5'89   TX840.F6

    ISBN 0-86188-064-1

Typesetting by Derek Croxson Ltd, Chesham, Bucks.
Printed by A. Wheaton & Company Limited of Exeter

Contents List

List of Illustrations vii

Introduction ix

Hints and Tips xi

Stylish Starters 1

Warmers and Coolers 13

Fish, Meat and Poultry Special 29

The Best of Fresh Vegetables 57

Salads from Everywhere 75

A Whizz of Sauces and Dressings 87

Nuts and Things 105

Dips for Dunks 113

Sweet Treats for Afters 119

Batters without Beating 135

Pastry without Tears 141

A Baker's Dozen — and More 149

'Quick as Lightning' Cakes and Biscuits 165

Flips and Shakes and other Drinks 189

Chutneys, Relishes and Marmalades 193

Acknowledgements 201

Index 203

Illustrations

Mexican-Style Avocado Cream Soup	Facing Page 36
Marinaded Stuffed Lamb	Facing Page 37
Avocado and Gammon Grill	Facing Page 52
Appetising Meat Plait	Facing Page 53
Cherry Brandy Savarin	Facing Page 148
Cheese Scone Round	Facing Page 149
Sticky Cinammon Bun Cake	Facing Page 164
Lemon Curd Tarts	Facing Page 165

Jacket Illustrations

Chocolate Layer Cake with Chocolate Butter Cream	Front Cover
Cheese Biscuits	Front Cover
Ian's Carrot and Courgette Soup	Front Cover
Country Liver Pâté	Front Cover
Salad	Back Cover
Red Cabbage	Back Cover
Rhubarb Chutney	Back Cover
Gooseberry Fool with French Biscuits	Back Cover
Brown Soda Bread	Back Cover
A Selection of Dips	Back Cover
Plain Scones	Back Cover
Patricia's Bakewell Tart	Back Cover

Introduction

'Many hands make light work' is, I believe, an old Chinese proverb but these days many hands are few and far between, and the next best thing to once-upon-a-time kitchen helpmates is the modern food processor which has the ability to cope with most food preparation techniques swiftly, cleanly and efficiently. Within the confines of one bowl, together with a metal chopping blade and a couple of shredding and slicing discs, you are all set to chop, grind, mince, purée, liquidise, blend and mix in a matter of seconds and the results speak for themselves. Ready-mades appear in quick succession and if you are as big a sceptic as I was when I first started out on this project (usually I am agin what I term 'new-fangled gadgets'), experiment with a few of the recipes and see what I mean.

When the idea of this book was originally discussed Patricia Hudson and I put our heads together and both agreed on what we ourselves would most want from a guide of this type; a blend of basic and traditional recipes interspersed and brightened with some new and inventive dishes for creative cooks of all ages. So that is exactly what we both worked towards and the choice is now all yours, be it a tangy Aubergine Soup spiced with cinnamon, a velvety smooth Cream Cheese Cake, feather-light Hot Cross Buns, delicious Ginger-Glazed Carrots, an original Cauliflower 'Slaw' Salad, unusual Sesame Meat Balls laced with green pepper, and down-to-earth Bakewell Tart served with cream or custard.

Speed and variety were, in retrospect, our main aims and we now have pleasure in presenting you with a book which has given Patricia and I many happy and easy hours of testing and eating. To save the effort of clock-watching, all processes have been counted where applicable, so if you have to process something for, say, 10 counts, simply count from 1 to 10 at a steady pace. Finally, a word or two of advice: ALWAYS follow the instruction book provided with your own machine and beware the metal cutting blade — it is very sharp.

Sonia Allison

Hints and Tips

1 Before using your processor, please read the manufacturer's instruction book. Familiarise yourself with all parts of the machine and its attachments. Put it together and take it apart several times before you actually use it.

2 Like all electrical equipment, a processor must be used with care; *always* ensure that the blades have stopped rotating before removing the cover.

3 *Do not* leave the processor running unattended.

4 Switch off the machine and remove the plug after use.

5 *Do not* allow children to use a processor and take extra care when using a machine if children are with you in the kitchen.

6 Always wash the bowl and blade or disc immediately after use, but never drop the blade or discs into a washing-up bowl. Use a long-handled washing-up brush or hold the attachment under a running tap. An old-fashioned bottle brush is ideal for cleaning the inside of the blade and disc shafts.

7 Only wipe the motor base over with a damp cloth and *never* immerse it in water.

8 Food processors are so quick in operation that it pays to collect together and weigh out all the ingredients you require for a dish before you start making it. Also see that herbs, spices and seasonings are to hand.

9 Food processors are a different type of preparation machine, so traditional methods and some traditional recipes have been adapted for their use.

10   We have tested all the recipes in this book and although we give a certain number of 'counts' when processing various stages of a recipe, until you get used to the machine do stop and check frequently to avoid over-processing the food.

11   If a recipe gives block (hard) margarine, soft (tub) margarine or 'softened' block margarine or butter, it is most important to use the correct one, as different fats can have an effect on the texture and finish of a dish.

12   Puréeing of soups and sauces can be done before or after cooking. If the total amount of liquid is over 5 ml (1 pt) when using a standard-size processor, or over 275 ml (½ pt) with a small-size machine, keep back most of the liquid and reduce the thick part to a purée then mix the two together; alternatively, purée the food in several batches. The machines are so quick that even when working in batches the task is completed in a flash.

13   Some machines have a maximum contents line indicated on the side of the bowl. Do not fill the bowl beyond this mark or some of the contents may spill over the centre shaft.

14   Some manufacturers say you can whip cream or whisk egg whites in their machines; others suggest using a hand or electric whisk for these items. Be guided by what they say.

Stylish Starters

Smoked Mackerel Pâté

A rich-tasting, delicious pâté which is at its best spread over fingers of hot toast. Its other plus point is that it can be made in under a minute!

Metal Blade

1 large garlic clove, peeled
1 tbsp lemon juice
1 tsp Worcester sauce
50 g (2 oz) softened butter
225g (8 oz) smoked mackerel fillets, skinned and divided into
    large pieces.

Serves 6

1   Place garlic, lemon juice and Worcester sauce into processor bowl. Run machine for 5 counts.

2   Add butter and smoked mackerel pieces. Run machine for a further 20 counts.

3   Spoon into a small bowl. Smooth top evenly with a knife. Cover with cling film. Refrigerate for 2 to 3 hours or until firm.

Kipper Pâté

Metal Blade

450 g (1 lb) frozen kipper fillets
4 large slices brown bread
Small handful of parsley sprigs
50 g (2 oz) butter, softened
Freshly milled black pepper
Juice of ½ medium lemon

Serves 6 to 8

1   Cook fish according to instructions on the packs. Cool. Flake with two forks, discarding any skin.

2   Break bread into pieces. Put into processor bowl with kippers and all the remaining ingredients. Run machine for 15 counts.

3   Add more pepper and lemon juice if required. Run machine for a further 5 to 10 counts, according to whether a medium or fine texture is preferred. Turn into a 575-ml (1-pt) serving dish. Cover with cling film. Chill for at least 1 hour before serving.

4   Accompany with lemon wedges and crisp brown toast.

Egg and Avocado 'Pâté'

Metal Blade

4 large hardboiled eggs
2 large avocados (they *must* be ripe but not mushy)
1 level tsp garlic salt
1 tbsp lemon juice
½ level tsp salt
Good shake white pepper

Garnish
12 black olives
6 to 8 thin slices of lemon

Serves 6 to 8

1　Shell eggs and place in processor bowl. Run machine for 4 counts or until eggs are coarsely chopped.

2　Peel avocados. Cut flesh directly into bowl in coarse chunks. Add rest of ingredients. Run machine for a further 10 to 14 counts or until the mixture holds together.

3　Spoon out of bowl and mound neatly on a serving plate. Stud with olives and surround with lemon slices.

4　Serve with hot toast or cream crackers.

Country Liver Pâté

Metal Blade

125 g (4 oz) fat bacon pieces, cubed
1 medium onion, peeled and thickly sliced
1 large garlic clove, crushed
350 g (12 oz) washed pigs' liver, trimmed and cut into slices
225 g (8 oz) pork sausage meat
1 Grade 3 (standard) egg
Salt and black pepper to taste
1 herb bag (bouquet garni)

Garnish

Parsley
Lemon wedges

Serves 6 to 8

1   Slowly fry bacon in its own fat until fat runs. Add onion and garlic. Fry for 7 minutes or until very light gold.

2   Add liver. Fry for a further 5 minutes.

3   Remove to processor. Add sausage meat, egg, seasoning and contents of herb bag.

4   Purée in short bursts. Do not over-blend if you want a coarse pâté. Spread smoothly in a 1-litre (1½-pint), well-greased ovenproof dish. Cover with lid or foil. Cook for 1 hour at 180°C (350°F), Gas 4. Remove from oven. Cool and chill.

5   To serve, turn out of dish and cut into portions. Stand on lettuce-lined plates. Garnish each with parsley and lemon. Pass hot toast separately.

Extremely Rich Chicken Liver Pâté

Marvellous to make using tubs of chicken livers — and if you're in an extravagant mood! A little goes a long way, and the pâté should be served with freshly made toast. If you like brandy and garlic, these can be added to heighten and enrich the flavour.

Slicing Disc

Metal Blade

225 g (8 oz) onions, peeled and quartered
125 g (4 oz) butter
1 large garlic clove, peeled and sliced (optional)
450 g (1 lb) chicken livers, rinsed and well-drained
¼ level tsp nutmeg
1 to 1½ level tsp salt
1 tbsp brandy (optional)   *Add bacon*
Extra butter

Serves 10 to 12

1   Using slicing disc, feed onions through processor tube. Melt butter in large frying pan. Add onions and garlic. Cover. Cook very gently for 20 minutes.

2   Uncover. Cook for a further 20 minutes or until onions are golden. Add livers. Fry over lowish heat, uncovered, for 25 to 30 minutes or until livers are cooked through.

3   Spoon into processor bowl, fitted with metal blade. Add nutmeg, salt and brandy if used. Run machine for 20 counts. Scrape down. Run for a further 20 counts or until liver mixture resembles a purée.

4   Spoon smoothly into a serving dish. Cool. Coat with a 1¼-cm (½-inch) thick layer of melted butter, which acts as an airtight protection.

5   Cover with cling film. Leave in refrigerator overnight before serving. The pâté will keep for at least a week in the refrigerator and can be frozen for up to 3 months.

Note
If preferred, block margarine may be used instead of butter but there will be a flavour difference.

Mexican Guacamole

Metal Blade

50 g (2 oz) onion, cut into large pieces
1 to 2 large garlic cloves
75 g (3 oz) green pepper, cut into large pieces
1 tbsp lemon juice
2 medium, ripe avocados
2 medium, blanched tomatoes, skinned and quartered
Salt and white pepper to taste

Serves 6

1   Place onion, peeled garlic and green pepper in processor. Finely chop, running machine for 5 to 6 counts.

2   Add lemon juice, avocado flesh (no skin or stones) and tomatoes.

3   Process until mixture looks like coarse purée; about 6 to 8 counts.

4   Season to taste. Spoon into a dish, 'burying' one avocado stone deep into mixture to prevent it turning black.

5   Spoon onto plates and accompany with ready-made tortillas or freshly made and quartered pancakes (see page 139).

Tuna Mousse

Metal Blade

198-g (7-oz) can tuna
150 ml (¼ pt) mayonnaise (page 96)
150 ml (¼ pt) whipping cream
Salt and pepper to taste
1½ tsp lemon juice
1 packet aspic jelly crystals (to make 275 ml or ½ pt)*
2 Grade 3 (standard) eggs
Cucumber slices and watercress for garnish

Serves 4 to 6

1   Place tuna, mayonnaise and cream in processor. Run machine until mixture is well-blended and purée-like; 2 to 3 counts. Add seasoning and lemon juice. Process for another 3 to 5 counts. Leave mixture in processor bowl.

2   Make up the 275 ml (½ pt) aspic jelly according to instructions on packet. Allow to cool. Add half to fish mixture and process for 2 to 3 counts. Spoon into a mixing bowl.

3   Separate eggs. Whisk whites separately by hand until they resemble stiff snow. Fold into fish mixture.

4   When beginning to set, divide mixture equally between 4 to 6 wine-type glasses. Top with a thin layer of the remaining aspic jelly.

5   Chill for 1 hour. Serve garnished with cucumber slices and watercress sprigs.

*If aspic jelly is unavailable, heat 150 ml water (¼ pt) with 2 heaped tsp pickling spice until it boils. Draw pan aside. Add 1 level tsp salt and 150 ml (¼ pt) mild vinegar. Strain. Pour a little liquid into pan. Add 2 lightly rounded tsp gelatine. Dissolve over low heat. Stir in rest of liquid. Use as directed above.

9

Marsala Pizza Squares

A gimmicky Pizza variation that appeals to young and old alike.

Metal Blade

Milk Pastry
225 g (8 oz) self-raising flour
140 g (4½ oz) butter or block margarine, cubed
3 tbsp cold milk

Topping
1 packet (227 g or 8 oz) Mozzarella cheese, cubed
2 tbsp Marsala
2 rounded tbsp tomato purée
1 Grade 3 (standard) egg
2 medium peeled garlic cloves
1 level tsp dried basil

For Sprinkling
3 rounded tbsp lightly toasted breadcrumbs
1 tbsp salad oil

Serves 8

1   Grease thoroughly a swiss roll tin measuring 30 cm by 20 cm (12 by 8 inches). Set oven to 220°C (425°F), Gas 7.

2   For pastry, sift flour into processor bowl. Add butter or margarine. Run machine for 30 to 40 counts or until ingredients resemble fine breadcrumbs.

3   With machine still running, pour milk down processor tube. Process until mixture forms a ball of softish dough in the middle of the bowl around the blades.

4   Turn out onto a floured surface. Knead lightly until smooth. Roll into an oblong large enough to line base and sides of the tin.

5   For topping, place all the ingredients in processor
     bowl. Run machine for 40 to 50 counts, by which time
     the cheese should be finely chopped and the ingredients
     well mixed. Spread over pastry in tin.
6   Sprinkle with crumbs, then trickle oil over the top. Bake
     for 35 to 40 minutes: the pastry should be crisp and the
     topping golden. Cut into squares or fingers and serve
     hot or cold.

Creamed Mushrooms

Metal Blade

Slicing Disc

1 medium onion, peeled and quartered
2 tbsps salad oil
450 g (1 lb) mushrooms
Salt
Freshly milled black pepper
Juice of 1 medium lemon
1 carton (142 ml or 5 fl oz) soured cream
Parsley sprigs for garnishing

Serves 4 to 6

1   Using metal blade, reduce onion to a purée in processor.
     Lightly sauté in oil in a large frying pan.
2   If necessary, peel and trim mushrooms. Halve large
     ones.
3   Using slicing disc, feed mushrooms through processor
     tube, pressing well down with plunger. Add mushrooms
     to onion. Sprinkle with seasoning and lemon juice.
     Cover. Cook gently for about 6 minutes.
4   Lightly stir in soured cream. Adjust seasoning to taste.
     Cook for 2 more minutes.
5   Serve in individual dishes, garnished with sprigs of
     parsley.

Warmers and Coolers

Golden Onion Soup

Slicing Disc

Grating Disc

450 g (1 lb) onions, peeled and quartered
25 g (1 oz) butter
2 tsp salad oil
2 level tbsp plain flour
1¼ litres (2 pt) boiling water
Salt and pepper to taste
50 g (2 oz) mature Cheddar cheese, cubed

Serves 6

1   Feed onions through processor tube, in three batches, pushing well down with plunger.

2   Heat butter and oil in a fairly large saucepan. Add onions. Fry gently, uncovered, until soft and golden. Allow about 15 minutes, but do not allow onions to burn.

3   Stir in flour. Cook for 2 minutes. Gradually blend in water. Bring to boil, stirring continuously. Reduce heat. Season to taste. Cover pan.

4   Simmer soup for about 30 to 45 minutes or until onions are very tender. Stir occasionally to prevent sticking.

5   To grate cheese, fit grating disc into washed and dried processor bowl. Feed cubes through processor tube, pushing down with plunger.

6   Ladle soup into bowls. Sprinkle cheese on top of each. Serve straight away while still very hot.

Chilled Dubarry Cream Soup

Metal Blade

Grating Disc

1 large cauliflower
2 medium, trimmed leeks, well-washed
275 ml (½ pt) milk
2 level tsp salt
150 ml (¼ pt) double cream
275 ml (½ pt) water
Pepper to taste
1 medium carrot for garnishing

Serves 6

1   Trim cauliflower, removing leaves and tough stalk.

2   Break head into florets. Coarsely slice leeks. Place in a
    pan with milk and salt. Bring to boil. Lower heat.
    Cover. Simmer until cauliflower is very tender.

3   Process to a purée in two batches; about 6 to 8 counts
    each time.

4   Pour into a bowl. Whisk in next three ingredients.
    Cover. Chill for about 4 to 5 hours in refrigerator.

5   Before serving, stir round and ladle into bowls. Peel
    carrot. Cut it into chunks. Place in processor tube.
    Shred, pushing down with plunger, for about 4 counts.
    Sprinkle on top of soup.

Chilled Avocado Soup

Metal Blade

3 large, ripe avocados
2 tbsp lemon juice
575 ml (1 pt) cold chicken stock, made from cube or powder and
    water
6 fresh chive strands
150 ml (¼ pt) double cream
1 to 2 level tsp salt
3 to 4 drops tabasco
12 to 16 thin slices unpeeled cucumber

Serves 6 to 8

1   Halve avocados. Remove stones. Reserve one. Scoop flesh into processor. Add lemon juice, half the stock and chives.

2   Reduce to a purée; about 10 to 15 counts. Transfer to a bowl. Stir in rest of stock.

3   Whisk in cream. Season to taste with salt and tabasco. Add reserved stone — this will prevent the soup from darkening. Cover.

4   Refrigerate for a minimum of 4 hours. Before serving, stir round and ladle into bowls. Float 2 slices of cucumber in each.

Jellied Beetroot Consommé

Grating Disc

1 can condensed consommé
225 g (8 oz) cooked beetroot, skinned
1 small onion, peeled and quartered
½ level tsp salt
4 heaped tsp soured cream

Garnish
1 Grade 3 (standard) hardboiled egg
Small handful parsley

Serves 4

1 Pour consommé into a bowl. Thickly slice beetroot. Place in processor tube. Shred, pushing down with plunger. Add to consommé.

2 Repeat with onion. Spoon over beetroot. Add salt. Mix vegetables into consommé.

3 Spoon into four wine-type glasses. Top each with soured cream. Chill for about 2 hours in refrigerator.

4 Before serving, grate egg and parsley for 2 to 3 counts in processor bowl. Shower over each portion of consommé. Accompany with hot toast.

New Year's Eve Soup

For something a bit different, serve this hearty soup meal to your guests on New Year's Eve.

Metal Blade

Slicing Disc

450 g (1 lb) onions, peeled and quartered
4 garlic cloves, peeled
50 g (2 oz) butter or margarine
2 tbsp salad oil
900 g (2 lb) lean braising steak, cubed
450 g (1 lb) lean stewing pork, cubed
225 g (8 oz) green pepper, de-seeded and quartered
450 g (1 lb) skinned tomatoes, halved
1 litre (1¾ pt) boiling water
4 level tsp salt
3 level tbsp Tandoori spice mix or mild curry powder
4 large bananas
2 cartons (each 142 ml or ¼ pt) soured cream
Powdered cinnamon

Serves 12

1   Place onions and garlic in processor bowl and chop finely, allowing 30 to 40 counts. Transfer to a large saucepan with butter or margarine and oil. Fry very gently over low heat until golden.

2   Add meat to processor bowl in four batches. Mince fairly finely, allowing about 60 counts each time. Add meat to saucepan. Brown over moderate heat, fork-stirring all the time.

3   Fit slicing disc into processor bowl. Feed peppers and tomatoes through processor tube, pressing well down with plunger. Add to pan with water, salt and Tandoori spice mix or curry powder.

4   Stir well to mix. Lower heat. Cover pan. Simmer very gently for 40 minutes, stirring from time to time.

5   Feed peeled bananas into processor tube, pressing well down with plunger. Add to soup. Simmer, covered, for a further 3 minutes.

6   Ladle soup into warm bowls. Add soured cream to each, then sprinkle lightly with cinnamon.

Chilled Watercress Soup

Metal Blade

1 bunch watercress
1 small garlic clove, crushed
1 can condensed cream of chicken soup
275 ml (½ pt) water
150 ml (¼ pt) single cream
4 tbsp dry white wine
Large pinch grated nutmeg
Salt and freshly ground black pepper to taste
Finely chopped parsley or paprika for garnishing

Serves 6 to 8

1   Wash and drain watercress. Break off thicker stalks.

2   Put watercress, garlic and soup into processor. Reduce to a purée; about 6 to 8 counts. Pour into a bowl.

3   Stir in rest of ingredients except parsley or paprika. When completely smooth, cover and chill in refrigerator for a minimum of 4 hours.

4   Before serving, stir round then ladle into small bowls. Sprinkle each portion with parsley or paprika.

Lettuce Soup

Metal Blade

1 medium-sized, round lettuce
50 g (2 oz) butter
2 level tsp cornflour
575 ml (1 pt) chicken stock (made with cube or powder and water)
1 to 1½ level tsp salt
Freshly ground black pepper to taste
1 Grade 3 (standard) egg yolk
150 ml (¼ pt) single cream
Scissor-snipped chives for garnishing

Serves 4 to 6

1   Wash lettuce leaves. Drain in colander. Coarsely shred.

2   Sauté in butter for 3 minutes. Stir in cornflour.

3   Add stock. Slowly bring to boil, stirring. Cover. Simmer for 15 minutes.

4   Reduce to a purée in processor in two batches; about 10 counts each time.

5   Return to pan, add seasoning and bring to boil.

6   Blend egg yolk and cream. Stir into soup. Cook for 2 minutes over low heat, stirring all the time.

7   Serve each portion topped with chives.

Ian's Carrot and Courgette Soup

A deeply orange soup, shaded with thin slices of green courgettes. Simple yet elegant and perfect for entertaining.

Slicing Disc

Metal Blade

¾ kg (1½ lb) carrots, peeled and cut into chunks
100 to 125 g (4 oz) onion, peeled and quartered
2 medium celery stalks, broken into pieces
1¼ litres (2 pt) water
1 chicken stock cube
2 level tsp salt
450 g (1 lb) washed courgettes, topped and tailed
2 level tsp cornflour
150 ml (¼ pt) milk
25 g (1 oz) butter

Serves 8 to 10

1   Place carrots, onion and celery (in several batches) in processor tube. Slice, pushing down with plunger.
2   Transfer to a large pan. Add water, stock cube and salt. Bring to boil, stirring. Lower heat. Cover.
3   Simmer gently until vegetables are very soft. Strain liquid into a clean saucepan. Cut courgettes into chunks. Place, a few at a time, in processor tube.
4   Slice, pushing down with plunger. Add to carrot water in pan. Bring to boil. Lower heat. Cover. Simmer for 5 minutes. Remove from heat. Leave on one side temporarily.
5   With metal disc in processor bowl, purée carrots, onion, celery, cornflour and milk until very smooth; about 20 counts.
6   Add to courgettes and liquid in pan. Stir well to mix. Bring to boil, stirring continuously. Simmer for 2 minutes. Stir in butter. Serve very hot.

Potato and Carrot Soup

Metal Blade

50 g (2 oz) butter or margarine
1 medium onion, peeled and cut into quarters
350 g (12 oz) potatoes, peeled and coarsely chopped
350 g (12 oz) carrots, scraped and coarsely chopped
1 to 2 level tsp salt
Pepper to taste
1 bay leaf
575 ml (1 pt) beef stock made from cube or powder and water
2 level tsp cornflour
250 ml (½ pt) milk
150 ml (¼ pt) half cream or single cream
Good pinch ground mace
1 rounded tablespoon chopped parsley
Fried croûtons

Serves 6 to 8

1   Melt butter or margarine in a large pan.

2   Add the vegetables. Fry, covered, for 10 minutes over low heat. Add next four ingredients.

3   Bring to boil. Cover. Simmer until vegetables are tender; about 30 minutes.

4   Strain off most of the liquid and reserve. Remove bay leaf and pour vegetables into processor bowl. Reduce to a purée; about 8 to 10 counts.

5   Place purée and reserved liquid back into the saucepan. Bring to boil.

6   Blend cornflour smoothly with a little milk. Add to soup. Bring to boil, stirring. Add rest of milk.

7   Adjust seasoning. Add cream and mace. Reheat briefly. Serve each portion sprinkled with chopped parsley. Pass croûtons separately.

Old Colonial Tomato Soup

Metal Blade

1 kg (2 lb) blanched tomatoes, skinned
350 g (12 oz) peeled potatoes, cut into chunks
175 g (6 oz) onion, quartered
1 medium, trimmed leek, well-washed and thickly sliced
3 rounded tbsp tomato purée
2 to 3 level tsp salt
2 tsp Worcester sauce
1 level tsp marjoram
2 level tsp soft brown sugar (dark variety)

Serves 8

1   Place tomatoes in processor. Blend to a purée, allowing 20 to 25 counts. Pour into a saucepan.

2   Finely grind up vegetables. This should take 30 to 45 counts, depending on the machine.

3   Add vegetables to tomatoes in the pan, together with the rest of the ingredients.

4   Bring up to boil, stirring. Lower heat. Cover. Simmer for 15 minutes. Ladle into bowls. If liked, sprinkle each serving either with grated Parmesan cheese or chopped parsley.

Spiced Aubergine Soup

Metal Blade

1 tbsp salad oil
1 large leek (225 g or 8 oz), trimmed and washed
2 medium aubergines (450 g or 1 lb)
575 ml (1 pt) beef stock made with cube or powder and water
3 level tsp salt
1 tbsp garlic vinegar
2 tbsp lemon juice
275 ml (½ pt) extra boiling water
¼ level tsp powdered cinnamon

Serves 6 to 8

1   Heat oil in a large pan. Thickly slice leek and washed, but unpeeled, aubergines. Add to the pan. Fry, turning often, for 10 minutes.

2   Stir in next four ingredients. Bring to boil. Lower heat. Cover. Simmer for 30 minutes or until aubergine is very soft.

3   Process to a coarse purée in two batches; about 6 to 8 counts each time.

4   Return to pan. Add remaining ingredients. Bring just up to boil. Ladle into soup bowls and serve very hot with warmed Greek-style pitta bread.

Mexican-Style Avocado Cream Soup

(see picture facing page 36)

Metal Blade

25 g (1 oz) butter or margarine
25 g (1 oz) plain flour
575 ml (1 pt) chicken stock made with cube or powder and water
1 tbsp lemon or lime juice
1 carton (142 ml or 5 fl oz) soured cream
2 medium, ripe avocados
1 level tsp onion salt
Salt and pepper to taste

Garnish
1 medium, ripe avocado
Extra lemon juice

Serves 6

1   Heat butter or margarine in a pan. Stir in flour to form a roux. Cook for 1 minute without browning.

2   Gradually blend in chicken stock. Cook, stirring, until mixture comes to boil and thickens. Simmer gently.

3   Meanwhile, halve avocados. Remove stones. Scoop flesh into processor. Add lemon or lime juice. Reduce to a purée; 8 to 10 counts.

4   Stir into soup, together with the onion salt. Season to taste. Bring just to boil. Remove from heat.

5   Ladle into bowls. To garnish, peel avocado. Halve. Remove stone. Cut flesh into slices. Sprinkle with lemon juice. Add to soup.

Note
Flavour and colour are spoiled if the soup is left to stand and reheated. It should be served as soon as it is made.

26

Five-Minute Mushroom and Tomato Soup

The freshest-tasting soup imaginable — and it cooks in 5 minutes. It is also slimming in that it contains no fat or thickener.

Grating Disc

Metal Blade

450 g (1 lb) trimmed mushrooms and stalks, washed
1 can (793 g or 1 lb 12 oz) peeled tomatoes in tomato juice
2 large peeled garlic cloves
1 level tsp dried oregano
2 to 3 level tsp salt
3 tsp Worcester sauce
1 tbsp lemon juice
275 ml (½ pt) water

Serves 8

1   Feed mushrooms through processor tube, pushing well down with plunger. Do this in two or three batches to avoid over-filling the bowl. Tip grated mushrooms into a large saucepan.

2   Open can of tomatoes. Strain tomato juice into the pan with the mushrooms. Stand over low heat.

3   Fit metal blade into processor bowl. Add tomatoes and garlic. Run machine for 10 counts until the contents are reduced to a purée. Add to the pan, together with all the remaining ingredients.

4   Bring to boil. Lower heat. Boil gently, uncovered, for 5 minutes. Ladle into soup bowls and serve very hot.

On-the-Spot Celery and Tomato Soup

Total convenience — two cans and a processor equals one good soup made in under a minute.

Metal Blade

1 can (397 g or 14 oz) tomatoes in purée or tomatoes in juice
1 can (298 g or 10½ oz) condensed cream of celery soup
1 chicken stock cube
275 ml (½ pint) boiling water
Salt and pepper to taste
Sherry

Serves 6

1   Place tomatoes and celery soup into processor bowl. Add stock cube.

2   Run machine for 45 to 50 counts or until ingredients are smooth.

3   Transfer to a saucepan. Add boiling water. Season to taste. Heat, stirring, until very hot. Ladle into soup bowls. Add a dash of sherry to each.

Fish, Meat and Poultry Special

Stuffed Mackerel

Metal Blade

Slicing Disc

4 medium-size mackerel, boned
1 large slice white bread
Half medium-sized bulb of fresh fennel, thickly sliced
1 small onion, peeled and halved
125 g (4 oz) mushrooms, trimmed and halved
Salt and pepper to taste
25 g (1 oz) butter
Parsley for garnishing

Serves 4

1 Wash and trim the fish. Dry with kitchen paper and lay out flat on a work surface, skin side down.

2 Break bread into pieces. Using the metal blade in processor, reduce bread to fine crumbs. Tip into a mixing bowl.

3 Change to slicing disc and feed fennel, onion and mushrooms through tube, pressing well down with plunger. Add to crumbs.

4 Season. Draw loosely together with finger tips then divide and spread stuffing over fish. Roll each up from head to tail, securing with cocktail sticks. Place in a 1-litre (1¾-pt) shallow, heatproof dish. Dot with butter and bake for 1 hour at 180°C (350°F), Gas 4.

5 Serve garnished with parsley and accompany with baked tomatoes.

Note
This dish is also good served cold.

Baked Haddock Portions

Metal Blade

Slicing Disc

4 frozen haddock portions, thawed
1 large onion, peeled and cut into quarters
1 tbsp oil
2 large blanched tomatoes, skinned and quartered
4 medium celery stalks
2 level tsps dried basil
Salt and freshly milled black pepper to taste
25 g (1 oz) butter
4 tbsps single cream
Paprika

Serves 4

1   Chop onion fairly finely in processor; 6 to 8 counts. Fry in oil until golden brown. Transfer to a mixing bowl.

2   Using slicing disc, gradually feed tomatoes and celery through tube, pressing well down with plunger. Add to the bowl, together with herbs and seasonings. Spread over the base of a 1-litre (1¾-pt) greased, heatproof dish. Place fish portions on top. Season.

3   Dot with butter. Cover. Bake for about 1 hour in an oven set to 190°C (375°F), Gas 5.

4   Coat with cream. Sprinkle with paprika.

'Stuffed' Fish Cutlets in White Wine

Metal Blade

75 g (3 oz) brown bread
50 g (2 oz) walnuts
½ level tsp dried tarragon
1 level tsp onion salt
2 heaped tbsp parsley (no stalks)
1 Grade 3 (standard) egg
2 tbsp orange liqueur
4 cutlets (each 175 g or 6 oz) cod or haddock
150 ml (¼ pt) white wine
50 g (2 oz) butter
2 skinned tomatoes, halved

Serves 4 generously

1   Break up bread. Place in processor bowl with nuts, tarragon, onion salt and parsley. Run machine until contents are fairly finely ground; about 10 counts.

2   Add egg and liqueur. Continue to run machine until stuffing begins to hold together. Take out of bowl. Divide equally into four pieces.

3   Arrange fish in a large casserole or fairly shallow roasting tin. Spread evenly with stuffing.

4   Pour wine into the dish. Trickle two-thirds of the butter over stuffing on fish. Add half a tomato to each, cut side uppermost. Coat with rest of butter.

5   Bake, uncovered, for 40 minutes in a oven set to 220°C (425°F), Gas 7. Baste frequently. Serve fish with the juices from the dish. Accompany with any of the potato dishes given in the vegetable section. Serve with peas or sweetcorn.

Provençale Cod (Brandade de Morue)

Made slowly and painstakingly with dried salted cod in southern sun spots, we in Britain are lucky enough to be able to fall back on easier-to-handle smoked cod fillet which, with a processor at the ready, gives a fair and speedy copy of the original. With its heady flavour and unusual texture, this Provençale dish will appeal to those who like something original, and it makes a warming meal when served with whole boiled potatoes.

Metal Blade

450 g (1 lb) smoked cod fillet, cooked and flaked (cooked weight)
2 medium garlic cloves, crushed
7 tbsp milk
5 tbsp salad oil (olive if you like the Mediterranean flavour)
Freshly milled white pepper to taste

Serves 4

1   Place cod flakes, crushed garlic, milk and oil into processor bowl. Run machine for 30 counts.

2   Scrape down sides. Run machine for a further 30 counts. Spoon into a saucepan.

3   Cook and stir over low heat until piping hot. Season with pepper and serve with freshly boiled potatoes.

Creole Chicken

An all-in-one dish which has a lively flavour and bright appearance.

175 g (6 oz) long grain rice
275 ml (½ pt) chicken stock (use cubes or powder and water)
1 × 2 kg (4 lb) chicken, cut into 6 joints

Topping
75 g (3 oz) green pepper, de-seeded and cut into strips
100 g to 125 g (4 oz) onion, peeled and quartered
50 g (2 oz) unsalted peanuts
225 g (8 oz) tomatoes, skinned and quartered
1 tbsp salad oil or 25 g (1 oz) melted butter
1 level tsp salt
1 small garlic clove, peeled

Serves 6

1   Place rice in a large oblong dish which is about 10 cm (4 inches) deep. Moisten with all the chicken stock.

2   Arrange chicken joints on top, skin side uppermost. Cover with lid or foil. Cook for 1¼ hours in an oven set to 200°C (400°F), Gas 6.

3   Meanwhile, place all remaining ingredients in processor bowl. Chop fairly coarsely, allowing about 10 counts.

4   Remove dish of rice and chicken from the oven. Coat with topping.

5   Return to oven. Leave uncovered. Continue to cook for a further 30 minutes. Serve with a large mixed salad.

Patricia's Speciality Fish Pie

Slicing Disc

350 g (12 oz) skinned cod or haddock fillet, thawed if frozen
Water
1 small bay leaf
4 to 6 peppercorns
½ level tsp salt
3 large tomatoes, skinned and quartered
125 g (4 oz) trimmed mushrooms and stalks
1 more level tsp salt
1 level tsp mixed herbs
2 rounded tsp drained capers (optional)
Cottage Cheese Pastry (page 147), chilled
25 g (1 oz) butter, melted
Beaten egg for brushing
Watercress for garnishing

Serves 6

1   Simmer fish until tender, together with bay leaf, peppercorns and salt, in sufficient water to cover; 5 to 7 minutes. Drain. Flake.

2   Feed tomatoes and mushrooms, in several batches, into processor tube, pushing well down with plunger. Tip into a bowl. Add salt, herbs and capers if used. Toss lightly.

3   Roll chilled pastry into a 35-cm (14-inch) square. Carefully transfer to a baking tray. Trim away jagged edges.

4   Spread fish over centre. Top with tomato mixture. Trickle butter over the top.

5   Dampen edges with water. Draw the four corners together to form an envelope shape, completely enclosing filling. Pinch joins carefully together between finger and thumb to seal.

Mexican Style Avocado Cream Soup
Credit – South African Avocados

Marinaded Stuffed Lamb
Credit – New Zealand Lamb

6   Brush with egg. If liked, decorate with leaves cut from pastry trimmings. Brush with more egg. Chill for 30 minutes. Bake for about 45 minutes at 200°C (400°F), Gas 6.

7   Leave to stand on tray for 5 minutes then cut into portions. Garnish each with watercress and serve hot.

Old English Kedgeree

Well-suited to brunch or lunch, kedgeree is an immensely appetising dish with origins in India, hence the curry powder. If preferred, use half smoked and half unsmoked fish; a combination of smoked haddock fillet and fresh cod is excellent.

Metal Blade

450 g (1 lb) smoked haddock fillet, cooked and flaked
450 g (1 lb) basmati rice (cooked weight)
4 Grade 2 (large) hardboiled eggs
125 g (4 oz) butter, softened
275 ml (½ pt) cold milk
2 level tsp mild curry powder (more if you like it stronger)
2 heaped tbsp parsley (minus stalks)
Salt and pepper to taste

Serves 8

1   Place haddock flakes and cooked rice in a large pan.

2   Place rest of ingredients in processor bowl. Run machine for 6 counts or until eggs are coarsely chopped.

3   Tip mixture into saucepan over fish and rice. Cook over minimal heat for about 30 minutes or until mixture is piping hot. Fork-stir frequently to prevent sticking.

S.A.F.P.B.—D

Monday Chicken Flan

Metal Blade

125 g (4 oz) Wholemeal Pastry (half quantity of recipe on page 146), lightly chilled in foil

Filling
1 medium onion, peeled and quartered
125 g to 175 g (4 to 6 oz) cold cooked chicken, cubed
25 g (1 oz) margarine, softened
25 g (1 oz) wholemeal flour
4 good-size parsley sprigs
1 level tsp mixed herbs
Salt and pepper to taste
275 ml (½ pt) milk
Juice of 1 medium lemon
2 tbsps single cream

Serves 4

1   Roll out pastry. Use to line a 17½-cm (7-inch) flan case and then stand case on a lightly greased baking tray.
2   Lightly prick base of pastry. Refrigerate flan for 15 minutes. Line with foil to prevent pastry rising as it cooks. Bake for 15 to 20 minutes in an oven set to 200°C (400°F), Gas 6.
3   Remove from oven. Carefully lift out foil. Return flan to oven. Bake for a further 5 to 7 minutes or until golden brown. Lift off flan ring.
4   Place onion in processor. Chop coarsely; about 3 counts. Add chicken. Chop for a further 6 to 8 counts until onion and chicken are finely chopped.
5   Add all remaining ingredients except lemon juice and cream. Run machine for a further 3 counts.
6   Transfer contents to a saucepan. Slowly bring to boil, stirring continuously. Cool slightly. Add lemon juice and cream. Mix in well. Cool.
7   Spoon smoothly into the flan case. Refrigerate until cold. Cut into wedges and serve with green salad.

Marinaded Stuffed Lamb *(see picture facing page 37)*

Metal Blade

2-kg (4½-lb) leg of lamb, boned
½ standard-size bottle red wine

Stuffing
50 g (2 oz) onion, peeled and quartered
125 g (4 oz) white bread, cubed
125 g (4 oz) dried apricots, well-washed
¼ level tsp dried thyme
¼ level tsp salt
25 g (1 oz) butter, melted
1 level tbsp clear honey or golden syrup
1 Grade 3 (standard) egg, beaten

Serves 6 to 8

1   Wash and dry lamb. Place in a glass or enamel dish. Coat with wine. Cover. Refrigerate for 24 hours, turning at least six times.

2   Before roasting, prepare stuffing. Place onion and bread in processor bowl. Run machine for 15 to 20 counts. Tip into a basin.

3   Cut in small pieces of apricots (use scissors for this), then add thyme and salt. Add the last three ingredients. Fork-stir to mix.

4   Drain lamb and pack with stuffing. Secure with skewers. Roast for 3 hours in an oven set to 180°C (350°F), Gas 4.

5   Cut into thick slices and serve with gravy made with the wine in which lamb was marinading.

Vegetable-Stuffed Lamb Shoulder

Metal Blade

Slicing Disc

About 1½ kg (3¼ lb) shoulder of lamb, boned
1 large slice white bread
3 medium celery stalks
50 g (2 oz) mushrooms
1 medium onion, peeled and quartered
3 parsley sprigs
Salt and pepper to taste
Fresh watercress for garnishing

Serves 6

1   Trim any surplus fat from meat.

2   Break bread into pieces. Using metal blade in processor, reduce to fine crumbs. Tip into a mixing bowl.

3   Change to slicing disc and feed the celery, mushrooms, onion and parsley through processor tube, pressing well down with plunger. Add seasoning and toss lightly together. Draw loosely together with finger tips to form stuffing.

4   Flatten meat and lightly season. Cover with stuffing. Roll up and tie securely with fine white string. Weigh.

5   Place meat in a baking tin and cook at 180°C (350°F), Gas 4, allowing 35 minutes per ½ kg (1 lb), plus 30 minutes extra. Remove from oven.

6   Place the meat on a serving dish and keep hot. Make the gravy in your usual way. Remove string before serving. Garnish with watercress.

Lamb Chops en Papillote

Slicing Disc

4 large lamb chops
1 medium onion, peeled and quartered
1 green pepper, de-seeded and quartered
1 head chicory, split in half lengthways and hard core removed
1 medium orange
Salt to taste
Freshly milled black pepper

Serves 4

1   Trim chops, removing excess fat. Place separately on pieces of foil which are twice the size of the chops.

2   Feed onion, pepper and chicory through processor tube, pressing well down with plunger.

3   Add a little grated orange rind and the juice of the whole orange. Sprinkle with seasoning. Toss lightly.

4   Pile equal amounts of mixture on top of chops. Enclose in foil, sealing edges firmly together. Place on baking sheet and cook at 190°C (375°F), Gas 5 for about 45 to 60 minutes, according to the thickness of the chops.

5   Fold back foil to show the centre of each. Serve in the foil.

Chicken en Papillote

Serves 4

Substitute 4 portions of chicken for the lamb chops.

Minted Lamb Patties

A tasty way of presenting lamb and especially appetising if served with fried potatoes seasoned with dried rosemary, and freshly cooked French beans tossed in butter.

Metal Blade

450 g (1 lb) lamb fillet
½ to 1 level tsp dried mint
1 large garlic clove
1 large slice white bread, cubed
½ level tsp salt
1 Grade 3 (standard) egg
Large pinch nutmeg

Serves 4

1   Remove excess fat from lamb. Cut meat into cubes. Place in processor bowl. Mince finely, allowing between 50 and 60 counts.

2   Add all remaining ingredients. Run machine for a further 15 counts.

3   Remove mixture from bowl. Divide into eight equal-sized portions. Shape into oval patties. Grill for 10 minutes, turning twice.

Stuffed Pork Shoulder

Metal Blade

Slicing Disc

1½-kg (3-lb) piece boned shoulder of pork
1 large slice white bread
1 large dessert apple, quartered and cored
1 large onion, peeled and quartered
3 level tsps dried sage
Salt and pepper to taste
2 rounded tbsp natural yogurt

Serves 6 to 8

1   Remove string from pork and open out. If necessary, flatten with rolling pin.

2   Break bread into pieces. Using metal blade, reduce to fine crumbs. Tip into a mixing bowl.

3   Change to slicing disc. Feed apple and onion through tube, pressing well down with plunger. Add to crumbs. Add sage and seasoning. Lightly toss together.

4   Add yogurt. Draw together with finger tips. Spread stuffing over meat. Roll up. Tie in several places with fine white string. Weigh.

5   Place in a baking tin and cook at 180°C (350°F), Gas 4, allowing 35 minutes for each ½ kg (1 lb) and 35 minutes extra.

6   Place meat on a serving dish. Make gravy in your usual way. Remove string from meat just before serving.

Pork Cutlets in Beer

Warming on a cold winter's day, and a hearty way of presenting pork.

Metal Blade

2 celery stalks, broken into pieces
1 medium onion, peeled and quartered
1 garlic clove (optional)
½ teacup parsley (no stalks)
1 small turnip, peeled and diced
4 pork chops, each 175 g or 6 oz
1 rounded tbsp flour
2 tbsp salad oil
1 bay leaf
275 ml (½ pt) beer
1 to 1½ level tsp salt
Freshly milled black pepper
Juice of 1 medium lemon

Serves 4

1   Place first five ingredients in processor bowl. Run machine for about 20 counts or until the contents are finely chopped. Take out of bowl. Leave on one side temporarily.

2   Coat chops evenly with flour on both sides. Heat oil in a large frying pan. Add chops. Fry briskly on both sides until golden. Remove to a plate for the time being.

3   Add vegetables to remaining oil in pan. Fry very gently, uncovered, until pale gold. Stir in bay leaf, beer, salt and pepper and any left-over flour.

4   Cook, stirring all the time, until mixture comes to the boil. Replace chops. Baste with pan juices and vegetables.

5   Cover. Simmer for 20 minutes. Remove bay leaf. Add lemon juice. Serve with creamed potatoes and peas.

Avocado and Gammon Grill *(see picture facing page 52)*

Metal Blade

75 g (3 oz) Cheddar cheese, cubed
75 g (3 oz) onion, peeled and quartered
1 medium-sized, ripe avocado
1 tbsp lemon juice
¼ level tsp salt
Shake of pepper
4 unsmoked gammon steaks
2 medium tomatoes, halved
Butter
Parsley for garnishing

Serves 4

1   Place cheese in processor bowl. Run machine for about 25 counts or until the cheese is grated. Tip onto a plate.

2   Add onion to processor bowl. Run machine for about 10 counts or until the onion is finely grated.

3   Halve the avocado. Remove and discard the stone. Scoop flesh into processor bowl. Add lemon juice. Run machine for a further 15 counts or until the mixture is fairly smooth.

4   Grill gammon steaks for about 8 minutes, turning twice.

5   Cover the steaks with the avocado mixture and then sprinkle with cheese. Top each with a tomato half, cut side uppermost. Dot tomatoes with butter.

6   Grill until cheese melts. Arrange on a serving platter. Garnish with parsley. Serve hot.

Potted Bacon

Metal Blade

1 small onion, peeled and halved
1 clove garlic, peeled and sliced
Small bunch parsley
2 small slices white bread
275 g (10 oz) boiled bacon
1 Grade 2 (standard) egg, beaten
1 level tsp dry mustard
1 bay leaf

Serves 4 to 6

1   Put onion, garlic and parsley leaves into processor bowl. Run for 5 counts.

2   Break bread into pieces. Add to bowl. Run for a further 3 counts. Turn the bread mixture into a large mixing bowl.

3   Cut bacon into pieces. Put into processor bowl. Run for about 5 counts until coarsely chopped. Add to mixing bowl with egg. Toss lightly.

4   Add additional seasoning if necessary, and dry mustard.

5   Turn into a 575-ml (1-pt) greased, heatproof dish. Place the bay leaf on top. Cover with lid or foil. Stand dish in a roasting tin containing about 5 cm (2 inches) hot water. Cook for 1 hour in an oven set to 160°C (325°F), Gas 3.

6   Serve hot with parsley sauce or cold with salad. Serve from the dish.

Party Ham and Chicken Risotto

A useful dish for teenage get-togethers. It is also economical if you use the meat from two or three home-cooked bacon knuckles.

Metal Blade

225 g (8 oz) onion, peeled and quartered
1 tbsp salad oil
225 g (8 oz) boiled bacon, cut into large pieces
225 g (8 oz) cold chicken, cubed
225 g (8 oz) American long grain rice
225 g (8 oz) frozen peas
1 level tsp dried oregano
575 ml (1 pt) boiling water
Salt and pepper to taste
Grated cheese

Serves 8 to 10

1   Chop onion finely in processor bowl, allowing about 5 counts. Tip into a large saucepan in which the oil has been heated. Fry gently over low heat until golden.

2   Place bacon and chicken in processor bowl and chop coarsely; 8 to 10 counts. Add to pan with rest of ingredients (except cheese). Bring to boil, stirring twice.

3   Lower heat and cover. Simmer for about 20 minutes or until the rice grains are tender and have absorbed all the moisture.

4   Fluff up with a fork. Pile onto warm plates and sprinkle each with cheese.

One-Pot Beef and Beetroot

An unusual combination of ingredients gives a special flavour to this economical and tasty dish.

Metal Blade

¾ kg (1½ lb) stewing beef, fat-trimmed and cubed
175 g (6 oz) onions, peeled and quartered
175 g (6 oz) cooking apple, peeled and quartered (core removed)
2 Grade 3 (standard) eggs
125 g (4 oz) pickled cucumber, thickly sliced
1½ level tsp salt
425 ml (¾ pt) water
1 beef stock cube
75 g (3 oz) wholemeal bread, broken into pieces
125 g (4 to 5 oz) pickled beetroot, thickly sliced

Serves 8

1   Place first six ingredients in processor bowl. Run machine for 45 to 60 counts or until ingredients are fairly finely minced.

2   Transfer to a saucepan. Add water. Crumble in stock cube.

3   Add bread and beetroot to processor. Run machine for 7 to 8 counts. Tip contents into the pan. Stir well to mix. Simmer for 45 minutes. Keep pan covered and stir occasionally. Serve with freshly boiled potatoes and green vegetables to taste.

Sesame Pepper Mince Cakes

Zesty meat balls coated with sesame seeds add a novelty touch to minced beef.

Metal Blade

675 g (1½ lb) *lean* braising steak, cubed
225 g (8 oz) onion, peeled and quartered
150 g (5 oz) green pepper, de-seeded and cut into large pieces
1 Grade 3 (standard) egg
50 g (2 oz) brown bread, cubed
6 rounded tsp sesame seeds
25 g (1 oz) butter or margarine, melted

Serves 6

1 Place one-third of the meat, onion and pepper in processor bowl. Mince fairly finely, allowing about 50 counts. Transfer to a mixing bowl. Repeat, mincing rest of meat and vegetables.

2 Add egg and mix in well. Place bread in processor bowl. Reduce to crumbs, allowing about 5 to 6 counts. Combine with meat mixture.

3 Shape into 12 hamburgers. Press sesame seeds on to both sides of each. Stand in a greased grill pan. Brush with melted butter or margarine.

4 Grill for 6 mintues under a pre-heated hot grill. Turn over. Brush with more butter or margarine. Grill for a further 4 to 5 minutes. Serve with chips or sauté potatoes and a large mixed salad.

Appetising Meat Plait *(see picture facing page 53)*

Metal Blade
1 packet (about 350 g or 12 oz) frozen shortcrust pastry

Filling
450 g (1 lb) lean braising steak, cubed
125 g (4 oz) onion, peeled and quartered
3 rounded tbsp parsley stuffing mix
2 level tsp prepared English mustard
1 level tsp salt
Good shake of pepper
2 level tbsp tomato purée
½ level tsp garlic powder (optional)
1 Grade 3 (standard) egg, well beaten

Serves 6

1   Thaw pastry. On a floured surface, roll it into a rectangle measuring 35 cm by 30 cm (14 by 12 inches).

2   Place meat and onion in processor bowl. Run machine for 30 counts. Scrape down sides. Run for a further 20 to 30 counts or until meat and onion are minced fairly finely.

3   Tip into a basin. Add the next five ingredients. Season with garlic powder if used. Mix all together with half the beaten egg.

4   Place pastry on a lightly greased baking sheet. Mark lengthwise into thirds, each 10 cm (4 inches) wide. Place meat filling in a sausage shape down the centre third.

5   Using a sharp knife, cut each of the other thirds into 1¼-cm (½-inch) strips to within 2½ cm (1 inch) of meat.

6   Fold strips over meat in criss-cross fashion, alternately covering the end of each strip with the next piece of pastry.

7   Seal ends and brush all over with the rest of the beaten egg. Bake for 15 minutes in an oven set to 200°C (400°F), Gas 6. Reduce heat to 190°C (375°F), Gas 5. Continue to bake for a further 30 minutes.

8   Cut into slices and serve hot with vegetables or cold with salad.

Meat 'Pie' Express

An appetising and economical mid-week standby dish that can be served hot with gravy and vegetables, or cold with salad.

Metal Blade

1 recipe Wholemeal Shortcrust Pastry (page 146)

Filling
450 g (1 lb) lean stewing beef, cubed
2 Grade 3 (standard) eggs
1 rounded tsp grated horseradish
1 level tsp onion salt

Topping
Beaten egg

Serves 6

1   Halve pastry. Roll each piece into a rectangle measuring 25 by 17½ cm (10 by 7 inches).

2   For filling, place meat in processor bowl. Run machine until the meat is finely minced; 45 to 60 counts. Add rest of ingredients. Run machine for a further 12 counts.

3   Stand one piece of pastry on a lightly greased baking tray. Spread with minced meat mixture, taking it right to edges.

4   Cover with second piece of pastry so that you have what is virtually an uncooked meat and pastry sandwich.

5   Score top of pastry with back of knife to decorate. Brush with beaten egg. Bake for 45 minutes in an oven set to 190°C (375°F), Gas 5. Cut into six pieces for serving.

Veal and Prune Loaf

A fine-flavoured meat dish, sandwiched with prunes. Serve it with freshly cooked pasta shells and lightly baked tomato halves. It is also delicious served cold with salad.

Metal Blade

450 g (1 lb) pie veal
225 g (8 oz) belly of pork (skin removed)
175 g (6 oz) onion, peeled and quartered
2 Grade 3 (standard) eggs
75 g (3 oz) brown bread, cubed
1½ level tsp salt
1 level tsp dried marjoram
1 rounded tbsp fine semolina
12 canned prunes (stones removed)

Serves 6

1   If the pie veal has not already been cubed by the butcher, do so yourself with a sharp knife. Repeat with pork belly.

2   Place both meats into processor bowl with onion. Run machine for about 60 to 70 counts or until the contents are finely minced.

3   Add all remaining ingredients except prunes. Run machine for a further 10 counts. Remove meat mixture from bowl and divide in half.

4   Spread one half onto a baking tray lined with greased foil. Using a knife, form into an oblong measuring 20 cm by 12½ cm (8 by 5 inches).

5   Arrange prunes on top. Cover with rest of meat mixture. Mark top into a diamond pattern with the back of a knife.

6   Cook for 1 hour in an oven set to 190°C (375°F), Gas 5.

Avocado and Gammon Grill
Credit – South African Avocados

Appetizing Meat Plait
Credit – Colman's Mustard

Terrine of Veal

This makes an ideal picnic dish when served with French bread, or as a lunch dish with salad.

Metal Blade

About 450 g (1 lb) pie veal (thawed if frozen)
1 small onion, peeled
3 bay leaves
3 sprigs parsley
Salt
450 g (1 lb) streaky pork rashers, cubed
2 to 3 garlic cloves, cut into pieces
1 tsp fresh thyme or ¼ level tsp if dried
1 level tsp finely grated lemon peel
Freshly milled black pepper
Ground nutmeg
2 level tsp powdered gelatine

Serves 6

1   Put veal, onion, 2 bay leaves, parsley and a little salt into a saucepan. Cover with cold water. Bring to boil. Skim. Lower heat. Cover. Simmer for about 30 minutes or until veal is tender. Leave to cool. Strain off and retain the liquid.

2   Put veal, uncooked pork, garlic, thyme, lemon peel and pepper into processor bowl. Run machine for 3 counts. Check seasoning and add nutmeg. Run machine again for 3 counts. This mixture needs to be chopped very coarsely.

3   Turn into a 1-litre (1½-pt) greased heatproof dish. Coat with 4 tbsp of the retained liquid. Place a bay leaf on top. Cover. Stand dish in a roasting tin containing 5 cm (2 inches) of hot water. Cook for 1 to 1¼ hours at 150°C (300°F), Gas 2.

4   Remove dish from water. Cover with a piece of foil and place a weight on top. Leave until cold.

5   Put gelatine and 4 tbsp of the veal liquid into a cup. Leave for 5 minutes. Spoon into a saucepan. Melt over minimal heat.

6   Pour over the terrine until the gelatine liquid just covers the top of the meat. Chill until jelly sets before serving.

Sausage Meat Crumble Slices

Just as good hot as cold and ideal for picnics or packed meals.

Metal Blade

Milk Pastry
Make as directed for Marsala Pizza Squares (page 10)

Filling
225 g (8 oz) pork or beef sausage meat
1 medium garlic clove, peeled
2 tsp milk
1 Grade 4 (small) egg

Crumble Topping
75 g (3 oz) wholewheat flour
40 g (1½ oz) butter or block margarine, cubed
2 rounded tsp poppy, sesame or sunflower seeds

Serves 8

1   Grease thoroughly a swiss roll tin measuring 30 cm by 20 cm (12 inches by 8 inches). Set oven to 220°C (425°F), Gas 7. Roll out pastry and use to line base and sides of tin.

2   Place filling ingredients in processor bowl. Run machine until the contents are well-combined; 8 to 10 counts. Spread over pastry. Wash and dry processor bowl and metal blade.

3   Place flour and butter or margarine in processor bowl. Run machine until mixture resembles fine breadcrumbs. Spread over sausage meat then sprinkle with seeds.

4   Bake for 40 minutes. Remove from oven. Cut into slices.

Devilled Kidney Pancakes

Metal Blade

1 medium onion, peeled and quartered
50 g (2 oz) streaky bacon, de-rinded and cubed
1 tsp vegetable oil
15 g (½ oz) butter
2 medium tomatoes, skinned and quartered
8 oz to 12 oz pigs' kidneys, cut into pieces
2 rounded tsp plain flour
3 rounded tsp French mustard
2 tsp Worcester sauce
1 tsp *each*, curry powder and Tandoori spice mixture
½ chicken stock cube dissolved in 275 ml (½ pt) boiling water
Salt
1 tbsp sherry
8 freshly made pancakes (page 139)
Chopped parsley

Serves 4 to 6

1   Place onion in processor bowl. Chop finely, allowing about 10 counts. Transfer to frying pan with bacon, oil and butter. Cook over gentle heat for 3 to 5 minutes.

2   Put tomatoes and kidneys in processor bowl. Run machine for 2 to 3 counts. Tip into a mixing bowl. Toss with flour and seasonings.

3   Add to onion mixture with stock. Cook over gentle heat for about 15 minutes. Add sherry. Adjust seasoning to taste.

4   Spread over pancakes. Roll up. Arrange on a serving dish. Sprinkle with parsley.

The Best of Fresh Vegetables

Brussel Sprouts with Bacon

A very appetising winter vegetable dish — delicious with roast turkey or capon.

Metal Blade

450 g (1 lb) Brussel sprouts
50 g (2 oz) lean bacon, rinds removed
75 g (3 oz) onion, peeled and quartered
50 g (2 oz) butter (unsalted for preference)
6 tbsp hot water
Salt and pepper to taste

Serves 4

1   Trim and wash sprouts, making a crosswise cut in the base of each. Leave on one side for the moment.

2   Cut bacon into pieces. Place in processor bowl with onion. Chop finely, allowing about 8 to 10 counts.

3   Heat butter in pan. Add bacon and onion. Fry until pale gold. Stir in sprouts, water and seasoning to taste.

4   Cover closely. Simmer for about 20 minutes or until sprouts are just tender. Avoid overcooking.

Ginger-Glazed Carrots

Chinese in style, try these carrots with pork spare ribs or roast duck. They are also delicious with a Christmas goose.

Slicing Disc

450 g (1 lb) carrots, scraped
1 beef stock cube
150 ml (¼ pt) water
50 g (2 oz) butter
1 level tbsp clear honey
1 tbsp lemon juice
½ level tsp ground ginger
¼ level tsp ground nutmeg
Salt to taste
Chopped watercress for garnishing

Serves 6

1   Feed carrots through processor tube, pressing well down with plunger.

2   Place sliced carrots into a saucepan with stock cube, water and 25 g (1 oz) butter. Cover. Cook for 12 minutes. Uncover. Cook over medium heat until most of the stock has evaporated.

3   Add remaining butter, honey, lemon juice, ginger and nutmeg.

4   Cook, uncovered, over medium heat for 3 to 4 minutes, tossing the carrot slices frequently until evenly glazed.

5   Adjust seasoning to taste. Spoon into a warm serving dish and sprinkle with chopped watercress.

Celery with Juniper Berries

Slicing Disc

1 medium-sized head of celery
150 ml (¼ pt) chicken stock, made with cube or powder and water
1 heaped tsp juniper berries*
1 level tbsp plain flour
2 tbsp milk
Salt and ground black pepper to taste
2 tbsp single cream
1 rounded tbsp chopped parsley

Serves 4 to 6

1   Separate celery sticks and remove leaves. Wash the sticks thoroughly. Drain. Cut into 10-cm (4-inch) lengths.

2   Feed celery through processor tube, pressing well down with plunger. Empty processor bowl when full and continue until all the celery is shredded.

3   Put celery into a shallow saucepan or large frying pan. Add stock and juniper berries. Cover. Cook over moderate heat for 7 minutes.

4   Blend flour smoothly with milk. Add to celery. Season with salt and pepper if necessary. Bring to boil, stirring. Cook for 2 minutes. Fold in cream. Sprinkle with parsley and serve straight away.

*These are available from speciality food shops but do need searching out.

'Quick Braise' Courgettes

Slicing Disc

450 g (1 lb) courgettes
4 tbsp chicken stock
¼ level tsp salt
Ground black pepper to taste
1 tbsp vegetable oil

Serves 3 to 4

1   Wash and dry courgettes. Cut off end pieces. Halve each.

2   Feed courgettes through processor tube, pressing well down with plunger.

3   Heat stock in a large frying pan or shallow saucepan. Add courgettes. Cover. Cook over moderate heat for 5 minutes, carefully turning courgettes twice.

4   Sprinkle with salt and pepper. Add oil. Cook for a further 1 minute. No longer. Serve at once.

Fried Courgettes

Appetising with grills.

Slicing Disc

450 g (1 lb) courgettes
Milk
Plain flour, well-seasoned with salt and pepper
Salad oil for frying
Freshly milled black pepper and salt to taste
Chopped parsley

Serves 4 to 6

1   Wash and trim courgettes. Cut into 7½-cm (3-inch) pieces.

2   Feed through processor tube, pushing down with plunger. Dip courgette slices in milk, then toss in seasoned flour.

3   Heat some oil in a large frying pan. Add courgette slices, a few at a time, and fry until golden brown on both sides. Turn twice. Lift onto a piece of crumpled kitchen paper on a wire rack. Cover with clean kitchen paper to keep hot and absorb oil.

4   Fry rest of courgette slices in same way, adding more oil if necessary.

5   Pile the courgettes in a serving dish and sprinkle with pepper, salt and parsley. Serve straight away.

Note
Courgettes cook quickly so allow about 1 or 2 minutes per side.

Braised Leeks

Slicing Disc

450 g (1 lb) trimmed leeks, halved lengthwise and well-washed
25 g (1 oz) fat bacon pieces, trimmed and cubed
2 tbsps white wine or stock
Freshly ground black pepper and salt to taste

Serves 4

1   Cut leeks into about 10-cm (4-inch) pieces. Feed through processor tube, pressing firmly down with plunger.

2   Put sliced leeks and bacon into pan. Cook over gentle heat for about 5 minutes, turning frequently.

3   Add the wine or stock and pepper. Cover. Cook over low heat for about 20 minutes. Stir occasionally.

4   Add salt if necessary and a little more pepper before serving. Serve in the liquid.

Stir-Fry Mushrooms with Onion

One of those simple vegetable dishes that is a splendid companion to meat, fish, cheese, poultry or egg dishes. The art is to be generous with the mushrooms.

Grating Disc

Slicing Disc

175 g (6 oz) onion, peeled and quartered
1 tbsp salad oil
450 g (1 lb) trimmed mushrooms and stalks, washed

Serves 6

1   Feed onion through processor tube, pressing well down with plunger. Transfer to a large frying pan. Add oil. Brown gently over low heat, allowing 5 to 7 minutes. Change to slicing disc.

2   Feed mushrooms through processor tube, pressing down with plunger. Add to onions.

3   Increase heat. Fry for 1 minute, turning frequently. Spoon out onto plates. Serve straight away.

Parsnips à la Crème

Elegant and finely-flavoured, the parsnips go beautifully with roast beef, lamb and poultry.

Slicing Disc

Metal Blade

450 g (1 lb) parsnips, peeled
Boiling salted water
50 g (2 oz) butter or block margarine, softened
4 tbsp double cream, heated until lukewarm
½ level tsp salt
Pepper to taste
¼ level tsp ground nutmeg

Serves 4 to 6

1   Cut parsnips lengthwise into quarters. Cut each length in half. Using slicing disc, feed through processor tube, pressing well down with plunger.

2   Cook parsnips in boiling salted water until soft. Drain. Transfer to processor bowl, fitted with metal blade.

3   Add all remaining ingredients. Run machine for 12 to 15 counts, by which time parsnips should look like a snow-like purée.

4   Transfer to a warm serving dish. Serve straight away while hot.

Parsnip Sauté

Slicing Disc

450 g (1 lb) parsnips, peeled and par-boiled for 5 minutes
Salad oil
Salt and freshly milled black pepper

Serves 4 to 6

1   Cut drained parsnips in quarters lengthways. Feed through processor tube, pushing well down with plunger.

2   Heat about 2 tbsps oil in a large frying pan. Add as many slices of parsnips as will cover the pan in one layer. Fry until golden brown on both sides, turning once. Repeat, using all the parsnip slices.

3   Remove from pan and drain on kitchen paper. Place in a warm serving dish. Sprinkle with salt and pepper. Serve very hot.

Pease Pudding

The traditional accompaniment to boiled bacon and very easy to make in the processor.

Metal Blade

450 g (1 lb) split peas
Water
½ level tsp salt
25 g (1 oz) butter or margarine, melted
1 egg yolk
White pepper to taste

Serves 6

1   Wash peas thoroughly. Soak overnight in sufficient water to cover.

2   Tip into a pan, together with the water in which the peas were soaking. Bring to boil, stirring. Lower heat. Cover.

3   Simmer slowly for about 1½ to 2 hours or until peas are soft. Stir from time to time to prevent sticking.

4   Also top up with boiling water if mixture seems to be drying out too much.

5   Remove from heat. Purée, in two or three batches, in processor bowl. Stir in rest of ingredients. When smooth and evenly combined, transfer to a well-greased, 1-litre (1¾-pt) casserole.

6   Reheat, uncovered, for 30 minutes in an oven set to 180°C (350°F), Gas 4.

Potatoes Savoyard

An exquisite French classic potato dish which, like the Gratin Dauphinoise on page 70, is child's play to make with a processor. Serve with fish, or with grills and roasts of meat, poultry and game. For vegetarians either of the potato dishes is suitable as a main course with salad or assorted vegetables.

Slicing Disc

900 g (2 lb) potatoes, peeled and quartered
1 garlic clove, peeled and halved
75 g (3 oz) butter, melted
4 rounded tbsp grated Parmesan cheese
Salt and pepper to taste
275 ml (½ pt) beef stock (made with cube or powder and water)

Serves 6

1   Feed potatoes through processor tube in several batches, pushing well down with plunger. Dry thoroughly in a clean cloth. Spread half over a well-buttered heatproof dish measuring 25 cm (10 inches) in diameter by 3¾ cm (1½ inches) in depth.

2   Crush garlic clove. Stir into butter. Pour half over potatoes. Sprinkle with 2 tbsp Parmesan cheese and season with salt and pepper to taste.

3   Top with remaining potato slices. Pour stock into dish. Coat with rest of cheese and butter.

4   Bake for about 40 to 45 minutes in an oven set to 220° (425°F), Gas 7, by which time the top should be crusty and golden. Spoon out of dish to serve.

Gratin Dauphinoise

Serves 6

Make exactly as Potatoes Savoyard, substituting boiling milk for stock. For an extra rich version, use boiling single cream instead of milk.

English-Style Cheese Potatoes

Serves 6

Follow recipe for Gratin Dauphinoise but omit garlic. Use 125 g (4 to 5 oz) grated Cheddar cheese instead of Parmesan.

Snow Potatoes

Airy-light and foamy, these potatoes go one better than creamed and, minus butter or margarine, are less rich.

Plastic or Metal Blade

1 kg (2 lb) potatoes, peeled and quartered
Boiling salted water
2 well-rounded tbsp dried milk powder
1 Grade 3 (standard) egg white (room temperature)
Seasoning to taste

Serves 6

1   Cook potatoes in boiling salted water until very soft. Drain, reserving 150 ml (¼ pt) water.

2   Place potatoes, hot potato water, milk powder and egg white into processor bowl. Run machine for 20 counts, by which time the potatoes and other ingedients should be well-mixed and very light.

3   Swirl into a warm serving dish. Serve straight away.

Hazelnut Potato Scallop

Excellent with poultry, or, with a crisp salad, as a meal in its own right.

Slicing Disc

Metal Blade

1 kg (2 lb) potatoes, peeled
1 medium onion, peeled
½ can condensed cream of mushroom soup
275 ml (½ pt) milk or water
Salt and pepper to taste
75 g (3 oz) Cheddar cheese
50 g (2 oz) hazelnuts
50 g (2 oz) butter, melted
Paprika

Serves 6 to 8

1   Cut potatoes and onion into largish pieces. Using slicing disc, feed vegetables through processor tube, pushing down with plunger.

2   Spread half the potato and onion slices over the base of a buttered, shallow heatproof dish of about 25 cm (10 inches) in diameter and 5 cm (2 inches) in depth.

3   Beat soup with milk or water until smooth. Pour half over vegetables in dish. Season. Cover with rest of potato and onion slices. Season again. Spoon remaining soup mixture evenly on top.

4   Fit metal blade into processor bowl. Add cheese and nuts. Chop coarsely, running machine for 2 to 4 counts.

5   Sprinkle over soup, trickle melted butter over top. Dust with paprika.

6   Cook for 1 hour in an oven set to 160°C (325°F), Gas 3. Spoon out of dish to serve.

Pan Potatoes

Akin to Switzerland's Rösti, this is a wonderfully sustaining cold-weather potato dish which tastes delicious with roasts of meat and poultry.

Grating Disc

450 g (1 lb) potatoes, peeled
1 large onion, peeled and quartered
50 g (2 oz) chopped streaky bacon or bacon pieces
2 tbsp salad oil
Salt and pepper to taste

Serves 6

1   Cut potatoes into pieces. Feed through processor tube, pushing well down with plunger. Repeat with onion.

2   Place bacon in a large and heavy-based frying pan. Add oil. Cook over low heat until bacon is crisp and oil hot. Add vegetables, spreading completely over base of pan.

3   Season and cover. Fry over a low heat for 10 to 15 minutes or until golden brown and crisp underneath. Using two spatulas, carefully turn over. Fry, uncovered, for a further 15 minutes, by which time the potato pancake should be brown on both sides.

4   Cut into wedges (or break into pieces) and serve very hot.

Ratatouille

The traditional Southern European vegetable dish that is now such a popular accompaniment to meat, poultry and egg dishes.

Slicing Disc

Grating Disc

450 g (1 lb) onions, peeled and quartered
2 large garlic cloves, peeled
5 tbsp salad oil
3 large unskinned aubergines, topped and tailed
2 large green peppers, halved and de-seeded
450 g (1 lb) courgettes, topped and tailed
450 g (1 lb) tomatoes, skinned
2 level tsp salt
1 teacup parsley

Serves 6 to 8

1   Feed onions and garlic into processor tube, in two or three batches, pushing down with plunger.
2   Heat oil in a large pan. Add onions and garlic. Cover. Fry over low heat while preparing other vegetables.
3   Cut aubergines into thick fingers. Cut pepper slices into wide strips. Cut each courgette into thirds. Quarter tomatoes. Feed all vegetables through processor tube, in several batches, pushing down with plunger.
4   Add to saucepan with salt. Stir well to mix. Cover. Simmer over low heat for 1 hour.
5   Fit grating disc into washed and dried processor bowl. To grate parsley, feed into processor tube, pushing down with plunger.
6   Add to ratatouille. Continue to cook, uncovered, for a further 30 to 45 minutes, or until very little liquid remains. Stir occasionally. Serve hot or cold.

Salads from Everywhere

American-Style Coleslaw

A mild and creamy salad which teams especially well with meat, poultry and fried fish.

Slicing Disc

¾ kg (1½ lb) Dutch white cabbage
50 g (2 oz) onion, peeled and quartered
150 ml (¼ pt) thick mayonnaise (page 96)
8 rounded tbsp natural yogurt
Salt and white pepper to taste

Serves about 8

1   Trim cabbage, discarding any outer leaves which are discoloured and bruised. Cut cabbage into large pieces.

2   Feed both cabbage and onion through processor tube, pressing firmly down with plunger. Tip into a large mixing bowl. Top up with cold water. Cover. Refrigerate for about 2 to 3 hours or until well chilled.

3   Drain in a colander to remove as much surplus water as possible. Dry in a clean tea towel.

4   Return cabbage and onion to a clean mixing bowl. Add all remaining ingredients. Toss well to mix, using two spoons. Pile into a glass serving dish before serving.

Coleslaw with Pineapple

Serves about 8

Especially good with poultry, game and cold boiled or roast gammon. To make, follow recipe above. At the very end, peel a small and ripe pineapple. Slice. Cut flesh into small pieces, removing and discarding hard core. Add to coleslaw. Toss.

Cauliflower 'Slaw'

A novelty salad in which cauliflower replaces the more customary cabbage. It is appetisingly crunchy.

Slicing Disc

Grating Disc

1 medium cauliflower, divided into florets
    (stalk and leaves discarded)
75 g (3 oz) carrots, peeled and cut into large chunks
1 small onion, peeled and quartered
4 rounded tbsp thick mayonnaise (page 96)
2 heaped tbsp parsley or fresh chives

Serves 6

1   To slice cauliflower florets, feed into processor tube, in several batches, pushing well down with plunger. Repeat the process with the carrots and onion. Transfer vegetables to a mixing bowl. Toss with mayonnaise.

2   Fit grating disc into washed and dried processor bowl. Feed parsley or chives into processor tube, pushing down with plunger.

3   Arrange cauliflower mixture in a serving dish. Sprinkle with parsley or chives. Chill for about 30 minutes in the refrigerator before serving.

Marinaded Cauliflower

Serve either as a salad or as a condiment to go with meat and poultry dishes.

Slicing Disc

Metal Blade

1 medium cauliflower, the head broken into florets
3 tbsp salad oil
1 level tsp prepared continental mustard
½ level tsp salt
¼ level tsp garlic salt
1 level tsp paprika
1 tsp mild vinegar

Serves 4 to 6

1   Feed florets into processor tube, in several batches, pushing well down with plunger.

2   Tip into a basin. Fit metal blade into processor bowl. Add rest of the ingredients. Run machine for 6 counts or until the mixture is smooth and well-combined.

3   Pour over cauliflower. Toss well to mix. Cover. Refrigerate for at least 4 hours before serving.

Tomato and Pepper Salad

A good one to serve with Mediterranean-style main courses.

Metal Blade

Slicing Disc

125 g (4 oz) American long grain rice, freshly cooked
150 ml (¼ pt) thick mayonnaise (page 96)
1 small onion, peeled and halved
4 large blanched tomatoes, skinned and quartered
1 each, medium red and green pepper,
     quartered and de-seeded
2 tbsp double cream
Salt and pepper
Juice of ½ small lemon
About 12 black or green olives for garnishing

Serves 6

1   Cool rice. Place in a dish. Cover. Refrigerate for about 1 hour. Stir into mayonnaise.

2   Using metal blade, reduce onion to purée; 5 to 8 counts. Work into rice and mayonnaise.

3   Fit slicing disc into processor. Feed prepared vegetables into tube, pushing steadily down with plunger.

4   Add sliced vegetables, with cream, to rice. Mix well. Season with salt, pepper and lemon juice.

5   Transfer to a salad bowl and garnish with olives.

Chicory, Cucumber and Tomato Salad

A pleasing salad to accompany pork and bacon dishes.

Slicing Disc

2 medium heads chicory
1 medium-size cucumber
4 large tomatoes, blanched and skinned
2 heaped tsp creamed horseradish sauce
6 tbsp French dressing (see page 99)
Freshly milled black pepper
Salt

Serves 4 to 6

1   Cut chicory in half lengthwise and remove hard centre core at base of each piece. Discard. Halve each length of chicory across the centre.

2   Cut cucumber into 7½-cm (3-inch) pieces. Remove strips of peel alternately round cucumber to give striped effect. Quarter tomatoes.

3   Feed chicory, cucumber and tomatoes through processor tube, pushing down well with plunger. Place in a salad bowl.

4   Beat horseradish sauce into dressing. When smooth and evenly combined, pour over salad. Sprinkle with pepper and salt. Toss lightly with two spoons. Cover. Refrigerate for 30 minutes before serving.

Cucumber and Yogurt Mousse Salad

Shades of the Balkans! Serve the Mousse Salad with poultry and egg dishes.

Grating Disc

1 small cucumber, peeled
142 g (5 oz) natural yogurt
Few drops tabasco
½ level tsp paprika
Salt to taste
2 level tsp powdered gelatine soaked for 5 minutes in
    4 tbsp cold water

Garnish
2 rounded tsp fresh mint, finely chopped
½ box mustard and cress, well-washed and
    cut away from roots

Serves 4

1   Cut cucumber into 7½-cm (3-inch) pieces. Feed into processor tube, pressing well down with plunger.

2   Transfer to a bowl. Combine with yogurt, tabasco, paprika and salt.

3   Spoon soaked gelatine and water into a small pan. Stir over very low heat until melted, but avoid boiling. Cool. Stir into cucumber mixture.

4   Refrigerate until just beginning to thicken slightly. Spoon into four wine-type glasses. Chill until firm and set.

5   Just before serving, sprinkle each with a border of mint. Pile mustard and cress in centre.

Middle-Europe Cucumber Salad

Slicing Disc

1 large cucumber, peeled
French dressing

Serves 4 to 6

1   Cut cucumber into 5-cm (2-inch) lengths. Feed through processor tube, pushing down with plunger.

2   Tip into a clean tea towel. Squeeze dry to remove surplus liquid.

3   Toss with just sufficient dressing to moisten. Pile onto individual plates. Serve with fish dishes.

Balkan-Style Salad

Serves 4 to 6

Prepare cucumber as above. Toss with yogurt. Season with salt and pepper to taste.

Waldorf Salad

An 'import' from North America — it is fast becoming as popular as coleslaw.

Metal Blade

About 4 large lettuce leaves
4 large celery stalks, broken
3 medium unpeeled dessert apples, quartered and cored
50 g (2 oz) walnuts
Mayonnaise

Serves 4

1   Line a shallow salad bowl or four individual plates with lettuce leaves.

2   Place celery, apples and walnuts in processor bowl. Coarsely chop, allowing 6 to 9 counts.

3   Transfer to a basin. Toss gently with sufficient mayonnaise to moisten. Pile over lettuce.

Dressed Mushrooms

Slicing Disc

Metal Blade

350 g (12 oz) button mushrooms, trimmed and washed if necessary
4 tbsp salad oil
2 tbsp vinegar
2 rounded tbsp thick mayonnaise
½ level tsp mustard powder
½ level tsp salt
1 heaped tbsp finely chopped parsley

Serves 4

1   Place mushrooms, in several batches, in processor tube. Slice, pushing down with plunger. Remove from processor and place in a mixing bowl.

2   Fit metal blade into processor. Add all the remaining ingredients except the parsley. Run machine for 4 to 6 counts or until the contents are well mixed.

3   Toss with the mushrooms. Pile onto four plates. Sprinkle each with parsley.

A Whizz of Sauces and Dressings

Basic White Coating Sauce (1)

Metal/Plastic Blade

25 g (1 oz) softened butter or tub margarine
25 g (1 oz) plain flour
275 ml (½ pt) milk
½ level tsp salt

Serves 4 to 6

1   Place all ingredients in processor bowl. Run machine until mixture looks like fine crumbs; about 15 to 18 counts.

2   Pour into a saucepan. Cook, stirring constantly, until mixture comes to boil and thickens.

3   Bubble gently for 2 minutes. Adjust seasoning. Use as required.

Basic White Coating Sauce (2)

Serves 4 to 6

This cooks more quickly than the previous method and it is hard to get it lumpy! Place 25 g (1 oz) flour into processor bowl with 275 ml (½ pt) cold milk. Melt 25 g (1 oz) butter or block margarine. When hot and foamy pour into processor bowl. Run machine for 10 counts. Transfer to a saucepan. Cook as Basic White Coating Sauce (1).

Pouring Sauce
Use half the amount of flour.

Sweet Sauce
Add 1 level dsp caster sugar to thickened sauce. Stir in only a small pinch of salt.

Parsley Sauce

Make Sauce (1) or (2) as directed. Stir in 2 heaped tbsp chopped parsley. Reheat. Serve with fish and bacon.

Mushroom Sauce

Make Sauce (1) or (2) as directed. Using slicing disc, slice 50 g (2 oz) trimmed mushrooms by feeding through processor tube. Fry gently in about 15 g (½ oz) butter or margarine. Add to thickened sauce. Serve with fish, meat, poultry, offal, egg and vegetable dishes.

Caper Sauce

Make Sauce (1) or (2) as directed. When thickened, stir in 1 heaped tbsp drained and chopped capers. Serve with lamb dishes, herring, mackerel or skate.

Mustard Sauce

Make Sauce (1) or (2) as directed. When thickened, stir in 1 to 2 level tsp prepared mustard and 2 tsp vinegar. Reheat gently.

Coffee Sauce

Make Sweet Sauce as directed above, adding 1 or 2 rounded tsp instant coffee powder to ingredients in processor bowl.

Chocolate Sauce

Make Sweet Sauce as directed above, but melt 50 to 75 g (2 to 3 oz) plain chocolate in milk *before* pouring into processor bowl.

Brandy or Rum Sauce

Make Sweet Sauce as directed above, but add 3 to 4 tsp alcohol to sauce after it has thickened.

Apple Sauce

Thoroughbred British and always welcome with roast pork, duck and goose.

Slicing Disc

Metal Blade

450 g (1 lb) peeled cooking apples, quartered and cored
3 tbsp water
¼ level tsp salt
1 level tbsp caster sugar
15 g (½ oz) melted butter (optional)

Serves 6 to 8

1   Feed apples through processor tube in several batches, pressing well down with plunger.

2   Transfer to a saucepan with the water and salt. Cook slowly, covered, until apples are very soft and pulpy.

3   Turn into processor bowl fitted with metal blade. Add all remaining ingredients.

4   Process until mixture resembles a thick purée; 10 to 12 counts. Spoon into a bowl. Serve warm or cold.

Bread Sauce

Metal Blade

50 g (2 oz) white bread (crusts removed)
3 cloves
1 medium onion, peeled
6 white peppercorns
Large pinch grated nutmeg
½ small bay leaf
2 small parsley sprigs, washed
1 small celery stalk, broken into pieces
275 ml (½ pt) milk
25 g (1 oz) butter
3 tbsp double cream
Salt to taste

Serves 6

1   Break bread into pieces. Reduce to fine crumbs in processor bowl, allowing about 10 to 12 counts. Tip out. Leave on one side temporarily.

2   Press cloves into onion. Put into a saucepan with all the remaining ingredients except the last three. Bring very slowly to boil.

3   Remove from heat. Cover. Leave to stand for 15 minutes. Strain milk into a clean pan.

4   Add crumbs, butter and cream. Season. Stir over minimal heat until piping hot and thick. Serve straight away with poultry.

Cheese Sauce

Shredding Disc

Plastic/Metal Blade

75 g (3 oz) mature Cheddar cheese, cubed
25 g (1 oz) butter or margarine
25 g (1 oz) plain flour
275 ml (½ pt) milk
Salt and pepper to taste
½ level tsp made mustard

Makes about 275 ml (½ pt)

1   Using shredding disc, feed cheese through processor tube, pressing down lightly with the plunger. Remove about 25 g (1 oz) if the dish requires a sprinkling of cheese for subsequent browning.
2   Change to plastic/metal blade. Add all remaining ingredients. Run machine for 3 counts.
3   Pour into a small saucepan. Bring to the boil, stirring continuously. Simmer for 2 minutes.

Instant Mint Sauce

Metal Blade

4 heaped tbsp mint leaves
3 tbsp cold water, chilled
3 level tbsp caster sugar
¼ level tsp salt
1 tbsp fresh lemon juice
2 tbsp wine or cider vinegar

Serves 6

1   Place mint, water, sugar and salt in processor bowl. Run machine for about 8 counts or until mint is finely chopped.
2   Add lemon juice and vinegar. Process for a further 2 counts. Pour into a sauce boat. Serve with roast lamb.

Onion Sauce

Metal Blade

2 large onions, peeled and quartered
275 ml (½ pt) cold water
Salt to taste
25 g (1 oz) butter or margarine
25 g (1 oz) plain flour
150 ml (¼ pt) milk
Good pinch *each* cayenne pepper and ground mace or nutmeg
2 tbsp single cream

Makes about 425 ml (¾ pt)

1   Place onion, water and salt in a pan. Bring to boil. Simmer, covered, until just tender. Drain well and reserve liquid.

2   Put butter or margarine, flour, milk, cooked onion and 150 ml (¼ pt) of reserved onion liquid in processor bowl. Run machine for 3 counts.

3   Pour into a saucepan. Bring slowly to the boil, stirring continuously.

4   Add cayenne pepper and mace or nutmeg. Adjust salt to taste. Finally stir in cream.

Low-Calorie Mushroom Spaghetti Sauce

Serves 6 to 8

Follow the recipe for Five-Minute Mushroom and Tomato Soup (page 27), but exclude water. Spoon the sauce over portions of wholewheat spaghetti. A sprinkling of grated Parmesan over the top of each portion is an optional extra.

Tomato Sauce

An economic venture, using readily obtainable canned tomatoes. A good sauce to serve with meat or fish, or over pasta.

Metal Blade

1 small carrot, peeled and cut into chunks
2 medium celery stalks, quartered
1 small onion, peeled and halved
25 g (1 oz) lean bacon
2 tbsp salad oil
1 × 400-g (14-oz) can tomatoes
1 level tsp salt
Pepper to taste
¼ level tsp nutmeg
1 bay leaf
2 tbsp tomato purée
Good pinch soft brown sugar
150 ml (¼ pt) water
1 level tbsp cornflour
2 extra tbsp cold water

1   Feed vegetables and bacon through processor tube, pushing well down with plunger.

2   Heat oil in a heavy-based pan. Add vegetables and bacon. Fry gently for about 7 to 10 minutes or until lightly browned.

3   Add tomatoes, salt, pepper, nutmeg, bay leaf, purée, sugar and water. Bring to boil. Lower heat. Cover. Simmer slowly for 45 minutes. Remove bay leaf.

4   Transfer contents of pan to processor bowl. Reduce to purée, allowing about 4 to 6 counts.

5   Return to clean saucepan. Add cornflour smoothly blended with extra water. Cook until sauce bubbles and thickens. Adjust seasoning. Serve hot.

Whole Egg Mayonnaise

A 'no-fail' mayonnaise with a delicious smoothness and fine flavour.

Metal Blade

2 Grade 3 (standard) eggs
½ level tsp *each*, dry mustard, salt and caster sugar
Large shake of white pepper
425 ml (¾ pt) salad oil
½ to 1 tbsp fresh lemon juice
½ to 1 tbsp mild vinegar
1 tbsp boiling water

1   Break eggs individually into a cup. Transfer, one at a time, to processor bowl. Add mustard, salt, sugar, pepper and 4 tbsp oil. Run machine until the mixture is well-blended; 4 to 6 counts.

2   With machine running all the time, trickle 150 ml (¼ pt) oil slowly into processor tube. At this stage the mayonnaise will have thickened considerably.

3   Add lemon juice. With machine running again, trickle in remaining oil. Finally add vinegar and water. Run machine for 2 to 3 counts.

4   Spoon mayonnaise into a non-metal bowl. Cover. Refrigerate for up to 2 weeks.

Notes
(a) The boiling water stops the mayonnaise from separating out.
(b) For half quantity of mayonnaise recipe and of all the variations — use 1 egg and 10 tbsp salad oil. Halve all remaining ingredients.

Mayonnaise Variations

1   *Cocktail Sauce*
    For all fish cocktails.

Add the following to every 275 ml (½ pt) prepared Mayonnaise
2 level tbsp tomato purée, 2 tsp lemon juice, 1 level tsp
paprika, ¼ level tsp cayenne pepper, 2 to 3 tsp horseradish
sauce or relish and 1 tsp Worcester sauce. For a stronger
colour and flavour, increase tomato purée by 1 or 2 level
tbsp.

2   *Garlic Mayonnaise*
    Favoured by garlic lovers with salads, roast beef, meat
    grills and roast poultry.

Add the following to every 275 ml (½ pt) prepared Mayonnaise
Either 1 to 2 level tsp garlic granules or 2 to 3 large garlic
cloves, crushed.

3   *Green Mayonnaise*
    Known in France as Sauce Verte, this is a distinguished
    mayonnaise packed with herbs. Ideally the herbs should
    be fresh but as this could be a limiting factor, and as the
    herb and spice manufacturers are now packing dried
    herbs which closely resemble fresh, I have used a
    combination of the two. Green Mayonnaise is
    particularly recommended for serving with fish.

Add the following to every 275 ml (½ pt) prepared Mayonnaise
3 rounded tbsp chopped parsley, 2 rounded tbsp chopped
watercress, 1 to 2 level tsp dried tarragon, 2 rounded tsp dried
dillweed and either 2 rounded tbsp chopped fresh chives or 2
level tsp dried chives.

4   *Tartare Sauce*
    The best known — and best loved — sauce for fried and
    grilled fish.

Add the following to every 275 ml (½ pt) prepared Mayonnaise
4 rounded tbsp chopped pickled cucumber or 2 level tbsp chopped gherkins (the gherkins are sharper than pickled cucumber), 2 to 3 level tbsp drained and chopped capers and 2 rounded tbsp finely chopped parsley.

5   **Thousand Island Dressing**
An American speciality, highly recommended for spooning over chunky green salads and hamburgers tucked inside warm, soft buns. It is also appetising with hardboiled eggs and shellfish.

Add the following to every 275 ml (½ pt) prepared Mayonnaise
1 Grade 2 (large) chopped hardboiled egg, 2 tbsp tomato ketchup, 1 level tbsp tomato purée, 12 finely chopped stuffed olives, 1 level tbsp very finely chopped or grated onion and 1 level tbsp chopped parsley.

6   **Tuna Mayonnaise**
Different from the usual run and appetising with cold cooked chicken or veal and with steamed and poached white fish.

Add the following to every 275 ml (½ pt) prepared Mayonnaise
1 can (98 g or 3½ oz) drained tuna and 5 small gherkins, both blended to a purée in processor bowl for 3 to 4 counts. Also fold in 2 tbsp single cream, juice of ½ small lemon and freshly milled pepper to taste.

Creamy French Dressing

This dressing goes well with a cold fish salad.

Metal Blade

Ingredients as for French Dressing (page 99)
1 packet (about 75 g or 3 oz) full fat soft cheese
   (such as Philadelphia)

1   Put the French Dressing ingredients into processor bowl and run machine for 3 to 4 counts.

2   Add the soft cheese and run again for 3 to 5 counts.

French Dressing

Plastic or Metal Blade

150 ml (¼ pt) salad oil
Salt and freshly milled black pepper to taste
¼ level tsp dry mustard
1 tsp lemon juice
1 level tsp caster sugar
4 tbsp wine vinegar

1   Put oil and seasonings into processor bowl. Run
    machine for 3 counts.

2   Add lemon juice, sugar and vinegar. Run machine again
    for 3 to 4 counts or until dressing thickens slightly.

3   Use as required. Pour rest of dressing into a plastic
    container with lid. Store in the refrigerator up to 2
    weeks. Shake well before using.

Green Pepper Dressing

This is a good dressing for a tossed green salad when served
with grilled steak.

Metal Blade

Ingredients as for French Dressing (see above)
1 medium-sized green pepper, de-seeded and quartered

1   Put the French Dressing ingredients into processor bowl
    and run machine for 3 to 4 counts.

2   Add green pepper and run machine again for 2 to 3
    counts.

Horseradish Dressing

Serve with cold roast beef or tongue and salad.

Metal Blade

French Dressing (page 99)
2 heaped tsp creamed horseradish

1   Put French Dressing into processor bowl.

2   Add creamed horseradish. Run machine for 3 counts.

Hardboiled Egg Dressing

This dressing is good served with cold chicken.

Metal Blade

2 hardboiled eggs, shelled and quartered
¼ level tsp dry mustard
Salt and pepper to taste
Shake of tabasco
2 tbsp wine or cider vinegar (light colour)
2 tbsp double cream

Serves 4 tc 6

1   Put all ingredients, except the cream, into processor bowl. Run machine for 6 counts.

2   Add cream. Run machine for a further 2 to 3 counts.

Avocado Salad Cream

An unusual dressing that is just right for spooning over hardboiled eggs, chunky vegetable salads and portions of fish or poultry.

Metal or Plastic Disc

75 g (3 oz) cream cheese
1 medium, ripe avocado
1 tbsp lemon juice
½ level tsp powder mustard
½ level tsp salt
¼ level tsp sugar
¼ level tsp onion or garlic powder
1 level tsp dried dillweed (optional)
2 tbsp milk

Serves 8

1   Place cream cheese in processor bowl. Peel avocado and cut flesh into chunks directly into bowl. Reserve stone. Run machine for 6 counts or until ingredients are smoothly blended.

2   Scrape down sides. Add lemon juice, mustard, salt, sugar, onion or garlic powder, dillweed and milk.

3   Run machine for 20 counts, by which time the dressing should be well mixed. Spoon into a dish and bury the avocado stone in the centre of the dressing to prevent it from discolouring.

4   Cover and refrigerate until ready for use.

Watercress Cream Topping

A cross between a classic sauce and a savoury butter, this topping came about by chance and is superb spooned over grilled foods, be they lavish steaks or modest sausages.

Metal Blade

50 g (2 oz) watercress leaves and thin stalks
15 g (½ oz) butter
150 ml (¼ pt) boiling chicken stock (use cube or powder and water)
2 level tsp cornflour
3 heaped tsp soured cream
Salt and freshly milled pepper to taste
¼ level tsp dried marjoram

Serves 6

1   Fry watercress leaves and stalks gently in the butter for 5 minutes. Transfer to processor bowl.

2   Add all remaining ingredients. Run machine until mixture is purée-like and smooth; about 30 counts.

3   Return to the pan in which watercress was fried. Cook, stirring, until it comes to boil and thickens. Simmer for 1 minute. Serve hot.

Brandy Butter Sauce

The traditional sauce for Christmas Pudding and warm mince pies. Rich and spicy.

Metal Blade

175 g (6 oz) unsalted butter, softened
75 g (3 oz) caster sugar
75 g (3 oz) sifted icing sugar
2 tbsp brandy
Powdered cinnamon

Serves 8 to 10

1   Place all ingredients (except cinnamon) in processor bowl. Run machine for 20 counts or until mixture is well creamed.

2   Spoon attractively into a small dish. Sprinkle lightly with cinnamon. Refrigerate for 1 or 2 hours or until hard. Spoon out of dish to serve.

Rum Butter Sauce

Serves 8 to 10

Follow recipe for Brandy Butter Sauce, substituting dark rum for brandy. Sprinkle with grated nutmeg instead of cinnamon.

Pineapple Sauce

This sauce goes well with ice-cream, baked and steamed sponge puddings and pancakes.

Metal Blade

1 227-g (8-oz) can pineapple pieces
1 rounded tsp cornflour
½ level tsp cinnamon
1 tsp lemon juice

Makes just under 275 ml (½ pt)

1   Tip complete can of pineapple, with syrup, into processor bowl.

2   Add rest of ingredients. Run machine for 3 counts.

3   Pour into a small saucepan. Bring slowly to the boil, stirring all the time. Simmer for 2 minutes.

Nuts and Things

Savoury Brazil Nut Slivers

Tempting party nibbles.

Slicing Disc

225 g (8 oz) brazil nuts
Shallow oil for frying
1 level tsp onion powder
½ level tsp salt
½ level tsp celery salt
1 level tsp paprika

Serves 8 to 12

1   Feed nuts through processor tube, pushing well down
     with plunger.

2   Heat oil in pan. Add nuts and onion powder. Fry gently
     until golden, taking care not to overcook as nuts brown
     rapidly. Turn often.

3   Remove from pan. Drain on paper towels. Toss with
     rest of ingredients. Leave until completely cold before
     serving.

Brazil and Peanut Stuffing

An appetising and slightly unusual stuffing, sufficient for the neck end of 2 chickens or 1 medium-sized turkey. If you are only using half quantity, freeze remainder for up to 6 months.

Metal Blade

50 g (2 oz) brazil nuts
50 g (2 oz) unsalted peanuts
50 g (2 oz) white bread (2 to 3 slices, depending on size,
     broken into pieces)
100 g (3 to 4 oz) onion, peeled and quartered
1 Grade 3 (standard) egg
½ level tsp salt
½ level tsp marjoram

1   Place first four ingredients in processor bowl. Run machine until the contents are fairly finely ground; 15 to 17 counts.

2   Add egg, salt and marjoram. Run machine until stuffing binds together; about 8 to 10 counts. Use as required.

Savoury Nut Crumble Topping

Useful as a standby for sprinkling over an assortment of savoury mixtures of fish, meat, poultry or vegetables in sauce.

Metal Blade

6 Ryvitas, broken up
125 g (4 oz) Cheddar cheese, cubed
125 g (4 oz) cashews or unsalted peanuts
½ level tsp salt
1 level tsp mixed herbs

Sufficient for 2 average-size crumbles.

1   Place Ryvitas, cheese, nuts and salt in processor bowl. Run machine for 15 to 18 counts or until mixture resembles fine breadcrumbs. Add herbs.
2   Transfer to an airtight container. Refrigerate until required.

Savoury Nut Stuffing

Makes a sufficient amount for the neck end of an average-size turkey or a large chicken.

Metal Blade

175 g (6 oz) white bread, cubed
75 g (3 oz) walnuts or a mixture of salted peanuts and cashews
50 g (2 oz) onion, peeled and halved
1 level tsp *each* salt, dry mustard and curry powder
1 Grade 3 (standard) egg, beaten
2 tbsp milk

1   Place bread in processor bowl. Run machine for 15 to 20 counts or until bread is in fine crumbs. Tip into a basin.
2   Add nuts and onion to processor bowl. Chop finely; 7 counts.
3   Add to basin with rest of ingredients. Fork-stir until stuffing holds together. Use as required.

Mixed Nut Burgers

A lovely way to economise on meat! Try these vegetarian burgers freshly fried with an interesting sauce and sauté potatoes. Or for summer eating, serve cold with a lavish salad of assorted vegetables tossed in a zippy French dressing.

Metal Blade

125 g (4 oz) unblanched almonds
125 g (4 oz) cashews
125 g (4 oz) hazelnuts
125 g (4 oz) onion, peeled and cut into pieces
175 g (6 oz) cold cooked potatoes, cut into chunks
1 Grade 3 (standard) egg
1 level tsp salt
75 g (3 oz) fine semolina
Oil for frying (sunflower for preference)

Makes 12

1   Place nuts, onion and potatoes in processor bowl. Run machine for 10 counts. Scrape down sides. Run machine for a further 10 counts.

2   Add egg and salt. Run machine for 30 counts. Scrape down sides. Run for a further 10 counts.

3   Turn into a bowl. Add semolina. Mix thoroughly. With damp hands, shape into 12 burgers.

4   Fry in hot oil until golden brown, allowing about 4 minutes per side. Drain on paper towels. Serve hot or cold.

Walnut and Garlic Dip

One of those special recipes that adapts itself to all sorts of circumstances. I tried it first as a dip with halved radishes and pieces of celery. Then as a cold sauce with hot roast chicken. Then as a topping for freshly cooked pasta. It was a success with everything and quite delicious.

Metal Blade

75 g (3 oz) walnuts
1 large garlic clove
142 g (5 oz) natural yogurt
2 generous tbsp double cream
¼ level tsp salt

Serves 8

1   Place walnuts and garlic in processor bowl. Run machine until nuts and garlic are finely ground; 15 counts.

2   Take out of bowl and combine with yogurt, cream and salt. Chill lightly before serving.

Walnut Marzipan

An unusual marzipan, which makes a change from the more familiar variety made with almonds. Use it for covering cakes under a layer of royal icing. Mould it into fruits. Roll it into marbles and coat with cocoa powder for the most luxurious truffles ever. Pack it into stoned dates for the Christmas tea table. Use it as a cake or swiss roll filling.

Metal Blade

225 g (8 oz) walnuts
225 g (8 oz) caster sugar
1 tsp vanilla essence
1 Grade 3 (standard) egg

Makes about ½ kg (1 lb)

1   Place nuts and sugar in processor bowl. Run machine for 15 counts. Scrape down sides. Repeat twice more.

2   Add essence and egg. Run machine for 15 counts. Scrape down sides. Run for a further 15 counts. Use as required.

Note
If rolling out to cover a cake, do so on surface dusted with sifted icing sugar.

Middle-Eastern-Style Walnut Marzipan

Instead of vanilla, use a few drops of rose essence.

Dips for Dunks

Taramosalata

The Greek 'dip' that has become an accepted classic. Using a processor really makes the whole exercise very easy; this version took about 1 minute to work together. Serve with warm pitta bread (oval in shape and hollow in the middle) which is now available in some supermarket chains as well as in continental food shops.

Metal Blade

2 large slices white bread (with crusts) cubed
75 g (3 oz) cod roe from a jar, or 175 g (6 oz) in a piece with skin
2 medium garlic cloves, crushed
7 tbsp warm water
1 tbsp lemon juice
4 tbsp olive oil (for characteristic taste)

Serves about 8

1   Place bread in processor bowl. Add roe directly from the jar or scrape roe in the piece away from skin.

2   Add rest of ingredients. Run machine for 30 counts. Scrape down sides. Run for another 30 counts or until mixture is very smooth and light pink.

3   Adjust seasoning to taste and spoon into serving dish.

Cheddar Cheese Dip

Rather rich but companionable with dunks of celery pieces, cucumber and radishes.

Metal Blade

175 g (6 oz) Cheddar cheese, cubed
1 carton (142 ml or 5 fl oz) soured cream
½ to 1 level tsp powder mustard
½ to 1 level tsp salt

Serves 8

1   Place cheese in processor bowl. Run machine for 20 counts or until the cheese is fairly finely grated.

2   Add all remaining ingredients. Run machine for 10 counts. Scrape down sides. Run for 5 more counts. Spoon into a serving dish.

Chivey Cottage Cheese and Pepper Dip

Serve this low-calorie dip for lunch or supper with dunks of crisp pieces of vegetables.

Metal Blade

50 g (2 oz) red pepper, de-seeded and cut into strips
1 generous handful fresh chives
1 tub (227 g or 8 oz) cottage cheese
2 tbsp skimmed milk

Serves 6

1   Place pepper and chives into processor bowl. Run machine for 12 counts.

2   Add cheese and milk. Run machine for a further 12 counts. Transfer to a serving bowl.

Spicy Mayonnaise Dip

Metal or Plastic Blade

150 ml (¼ pt) *thick* mayonnaise (page 96)
4 rounded tbsp natural yogurt
½ level tsp onion salt
2 tsp tomato purée
2 tsp prepared mild mustard
2 tsp lemon juice
½ level tsp cinnamon

Serves 6 to 8

1   Place all ingredients in processor bowl. Run machine until the contents are smooth and evenly combined; 10 to 12 counts.

2   Scrape down bowl. Run machine for a further 5 counts. Spoon into a serving dish. Serve with dunks of cubed boiled bacon and cocktail sausages.

Bean and Horseradish Dip

Economical and flavoursome. Serve with dunks of celery and cucumber slices as a lunchtime snack or with drinks in the evening.

Metal Blade

1 can (425 g or 15 oz) butter beans, drained
3 rounded tsp Burgess creamed horseradish
1 tbsp mild vinegar
1 small garlic clove, peeled and sliced
1 tbsp water
¼ level tsp salt
Cayenne pepper

1   Place all ingredients in processor bowl. Run machine for 30 counts or until the mixture resembles a smooth purée.

2   Spoon into a dish. Dust very lightly with cayenne pepper.

Sweet Treats for Afters

Banana Spice Pudding

A moist pudding, bordering on the soggy, which everyone finds delicious! Serve it with single cream or custard.

Metal Blade

125 g (4 oz) self-raising flour
125 g (4 oz) caster sugar
1 level tsp mixed spice
2 Grade 3 (standard) eggs
125 g (4 oz) butter, melted
2 large bananas, peeled and broken up into large pieces

Serves 4 to 6

1   Grease thoroughly a 1½-litre (2½-pt) pie dish. Set oven to 180°C (350°F), Gas 4.

2   Place all ingredients in processor bowl. Run machine for 25 counts or until mixture is smooth and no large pieces of banana remain.

3   Transfer to the prepared dish. Bake for 1 hour, by which time the pudding should be well-risen and golden. Spoon onto warm plates and serve straight away.

Baked Autumn Pudding

A delicious family pudding which is juicy and full of flavour.

Metal Blade

Slicing Disc

2 large slices wholemeal bread
450 g (1 lb) peeled cooking apples, quartered and cored
2 medium-size oranges, peeled and divided into quarters
25 to 50 g (1 to 2 oz) soft brown sugar (dark variety)
1 level tsp cinnamon
50 g (2 oz) butter

Serves 4

1 Break bread into pieces. Using metal blade, reduce to fine crumbs in processor. Leave in bowl.

2 Change to slicing disc. Feed fruit through processor tube, pressing well down with plunger.

3 Transfer fruit and crumb mixture to a large mixing bowl. Add sugar and cinnamon. Toss lightly.

4 Spread evenly into a lightly-buttered 1-litre (1¾-pt) dish. Dot with butter and bake at 190°C (375°F),Gas 5 for 50 minutes. Serve with thick cream.

Guards' Pudding

Metal Blade

3 large slices brown bread
75 g (3 oz) soft brown sugar (dark variety)
3 level tbsp plum jam
3 Grade 3 (standard) eggs, separated
¼ level tsp bicarbonate of soda
15 g (½ oz) butter

Serves 4

1   Break bread into pieces. Put into processor bowl.
    Reduce bread to fine crumbs.

2   Add all other ingredients, except egg whites, and run
    machine for 3 to 5 counts. Transfer to a mixing bowl.

3   Whisk egg whites separately and fold into breadcrumb
    mixture.

4   Smooth into a well-buttered 1-litre (1¼-pt) heatproof
    dish. Bake for about 30 to 35 minutes in an oven set to
    190° C (375°F), Gas 5. The pudding is cooked when it is
    well-risen and springy to the touch. Serve with cream.

Steamed Coffee Sponge Pudding

A moist, golden pudding adored by all the family.

Plastic or Metal Blade

125 g (4 oz) soft margarine
125 g (4 oz) caster sugar
175 g (6 oz) self-raising flour
2 Grade 3 (standard) eggs
2 tbsp coffee and chicory essence
½ level tsp baking powder

Serves 6

1   Grease thoroughly a 1-litre (1¼-pt) pudding basin. Have ready a large saucepan and a kettle of boiling water.

2   Place all pudding ingredients in processor bowl. Run machine for 10 to 12 counts or until ingredients are well mixed.

3   Transfer to the prepared basin. Cover with a double thickness of buttered foil or greaseproof paper. Secure with string.

4   Stand basin in the saucepan. Add enough boiling water to come halfway up sides. Cover with lid. Steam for 1½ hours.

5   Turn out of basin onto a warm serving dish. Cut into wedges and serve with cream, custard or Coffee Sauce (page 90).

Baked Coffee Pudding

Serves 6 generously

By using softened butter and adding an extra egg, you can produce a feather-light baked pudding which is economical to make if you have the oven going for other dishes at the same time. Place all ingredients into processor bowl fitted with metal blade, adding 1 level tsp baking powder instead of ½ tsp. Run machine for 10 to 12 counts. Spoon evenly into a 1¼-litre (2-pt) buttered heatproof dish. Bake for 1 hour at 180°C (350°F), Gas 4. Turn out onto a warm serving dish, cut into wedges and serve with single cream.

Deep Southern Apple Pie

Metal Blade

Slicing Disc

225 g (8 oz) self-raising flour
Pinch salt
125 g (4 oz) white cooking fat, block margarine or lard
2 to 3 tbsp cold water
450 g (1 lb) cooking apples (such as Bramleys)
½ level tsp cinnamon
75 g (3 oz) soft brown sugar (light variety)
50 g (2 oz) raisins
1 rounded tbsp orange marmalade
Knob butter
Icing sugar

Serves 4

1   Sieve together flour and salt. Place in processor bowl. Add fat, cut into cubes.

2   Process until the mixture looks like fine breadcrumbs; about 15 counts. Do not over-process.

3   Add water and run machine for a further 5 to 6 counts, by which time the pastry should hold together. Knead lightly until smooth.

4   Foil-wrap and chill in refrigerator for about 30 minutes.

5   Peel, quarter and core apples. Change to slicing disc. Feed apples through processor tube, pressing well down with plunger.

6   Cook apples to a pulp in a covered pan with cinnamon and 1 tbsp water. Add sugar, raisins, marmalade and butter. Mix well. Cool.

7   Divide pastry into two. Use half to line a 20-cm (8-inch) pie plate. Dampen edges. Cover with apple pulp. Top with a lid cut from the remaining pastry. Make two slits in the top to allow steam to escape. Bake at 200°C (400°F), Gas 6 for about 35 to 40 minutes or until pastry is golden brown.

8   Dust with icing sugar before serving. Accompany with cream.

Pear and Honey Pancakes

Metal Blade

3 large and firm dessert pears
2 tbsp clear honey
¼ level tsp ground ginger
25 g (1 oz) walnuts
4 tbsp water
Lemon juice
Freshly made galettes or brown pancakes (page 137)
Icing sugar

Allow 2 per person

1   Peel, core and quarter pears.

2   Place pears, honey, spice, walnuts and water in processor bowl and run for 5 counts.

3   Transfer to a small saucepan. Bring slowly to boil. Cook for about 2 minutes. Add lemon juice to taste.

4   Dredge a little icing sugar over each pancake and roll up. Arrange on a serving dish. Coat with pear and honey mixture. Serve at once.

Patricia's Bakewell Tart

An economical version of a Derbyshire favourite.

Plastic or Metal Blade

Half recipe Shortcrust Pastry (page 143)
2 heaped tbsp plum or raspberry jam

Filling
75 g (3 oz) soft margarine
75 g (3 oz) caster sugar
50 g (2 oz) ground rice
¼ tsp almond essence
1 Grade 3 (standard) egg

Serves 6

1   Roll out pastry and use to line an 18-cm (7-inch) fluted flan ring, which is standing on a lightly greased baking tray. Chill again for 10 minutes. Spread jam over pastry base. Put margarine and sugar into processor bowl. Run machine 15 to 20 counts.

2   Add ground rice, essence and egg. Run machine again for 2 more counts. Spread filling over jam.

3   Bake for about 30 to 40 minutes in an oven set to 190°C (375°F), Gas 5. At this stage the top of tart and pastry should be a warm gold.

4   Leave for 10 minutes. Remove flan ring carefully. Cut tart into wedges. Serve hot with cream or custard. If preferred, cool tart on cooling tray. Cut into wedges and serve cold.

Traditional Bakewell Tart

In the old-fashioned style, this version of the Bakewell is a little bit extravagant but worth considering for special occasions.

Plastic or Metal Blade

Half recipe Shortcrust Pastry (page 143)
2 level tbsp raspberry jam

Filling
50 g (2 oz) butter, softened
50 g (2 oz) caster sugar
1 Grade 3 (standard) egg
75 g (3 oz) ground almonds
75 g (3 oz) stale cake (such as Madeira) broken into pieces
Finely grated peel and juice of 1 small lemon
¼ tsp almond essence

Serves 6

1   Roll out pastry. Use to line an 18-cm (7-inch) deep pie plate with rim, making sure pastry covers rim. Trim away surplus. Ridge with fork or pinch up between finger and thumb to decorate.

2   Spread jam over base of pastry. For filling, place all ingredients in processor bowl. Run machine for 22 to 25 counts or until the contents are well mixed.

3   Spread smoothly into flan. Bake for 20 minutes in an oven set to 220°C (425°F), Gas 7. Reduce to 160°C (325°F), Gas 3. Bake for a further 30 to 40 minutes or until filling is firm and tart is golden.

4   Remove from oven. Carefully lift off flan ring. Cut tart into wedges and serve warm with cream. Alternatively, cool on wire rack and serve cold.

Bakewell Tart with Lemon Curd
In earlier times, lemon curd was used instead of jam.

Cherry Brandy Savarin *(see picture facing page 148)*

Classic and elegant.

Metal/Plastic Blade

Yeast Liquid
3 tbsp boiling milk
3 tbsp cold milk
1 level tsp caster sugar
25 g (1 oz) fresh yeast or 1 level tbsp dried yeast
50 g (2 oz) plain flour

Other Ingredients
175 g (6 oz) plain flour
½ level tsp salt
25 g (1 oz) caster sugar
4 Grade 3 (standard) eggs, beaten
125 g (4 oz) butter, softened

Cherry Brandy Syrup
225 g (8 oz) granulated sugar
275 ml (½ pt) boiling water
4 tbsp cherry brandy

Filling
1 can (425 g or 15 oz) black or red cherries, drained
25 g (1 oz) flaked and toasted almonds

Serves 6

1   For yeast liquid, stir all ingredients well together in large
    bowl. Cover. Leave in a warm place for about 20
    minutes or until frothy.

2   Sift flour and salt into processor bowl. Add sugar, eggs,
    butter and yeast liquid. Run machine for 20 counts.
    Scrape down sides. Run for a further 20 counts.

3   Brush a 20- to 22½-cm (8- to 9-inch) ring mould with melted white cooking fat. Dust *very lightly* with baking powder to prevent the savarin from sticking.

4   Pour yeast mixture into the prepared tin. Cover with greased paper. Leave to rise in a warm place until it reaches the top of the tin. Uncover.

5   Bake for 25 to 30 minutes (or until golden brown) in an oven set to 200°C (400°F), Gas 6.

6   Meanwhile, make syrup. Place sugar in pan. Add water. Heat slowly until sugar dissolves. Boil briskly for 1 minute. Remove from heat. Stir in cherry brandy.

7   Remove the savarin from oven. Cool off slightly. Turn out onto a large serving dish. Pierce all over with fork. Saturate with syrup.

8   Stone cherries. Toss with any leftover syrup. Use to fill centre of the savarin. Scatter with almonds and, if there are any left, decorate edge with a border of cherries.

Strawberry Mousse

Metal Blade

½ kg (1 lb) strawberries
5 level tsp gelatine
4 tbsp cold water or 2 tbsp water and 2 tbsp Cointreau
3 Grade 2 (large) eggs, separated
125 g (4 oz) caster sugar
150 ml (¼ pt) double cream

Decoration
125 g (4 oz) extra strawberries, sliced

Serves 8

1   Wash and hull strawberries. Place in processor bowl. Run machine for about 8 to 10 counts or until fruit forms a thick and smooth purée.

2   Shower gelatine into cold water. Leave to stand for 3 minutes. Spoon into a small pan. Melt over very low heat. Add to strawberry purée in processor bowl together with Cointreau (if used) and egg yolks.

3   Process for 2 to 3 counts or until ingredients are well mixed. Pour into a clean basin. Cover. Refrigerate until just beginning to firm up and thicken.

4   Beat egg whites to a stiff snow. Add sugar. Continue to beat until mixture is very heavy and stiffer than it was before. Whip cream until thick.

5   Fold beaten whites and sugar into strawberry purée alternately with whipped cream. Continue to flip mixture over and over on itself until evenly combined.

6   Pour into a glass serving bowl and refrigerate until set. Before serving, decorate with sliced strawberries.

Luxury Fruit Fool

One of the old standbys that never loses its appeal.

Metal Blade

450 g (1 lb) gooseberries, topped and tailed
3 tbsp water
3 rounded tbsp granulated sugar
½ tsp vanilla essence (which brings out flavour of fruit)
½ level tsp finely grated lemon peel
150 ml (¼ pt) double cream

Serves 4

1   Place gooseberries and water in a pan. Bring to boil.
     Lower heat. Cover. Cook very slowly for 10 minutes or
     until fruit is soft and pulpy.

2   Tip into processor bowl. Add sugar, essence and lemon
     peel. Run machine for 20 counts. Scrape down sides.

3   Run machine for a further 30 counts. Pour purée into
     basin. Cover. Leave until completely cold.

4   Whip cream until thick. Gently whisk in cold fruit
     purée. When smooth and evenly combined, transfer to
     four sundae glasses.

5   Chill lightly before serving with crisp biscuits.

Rhubarb Fruit Fool

Serves 4

Make exactly as the Luxury Fruit Fool, substituting 450 g
(1 lb) cut-up rhubarb (prepared weight) for the gooseberries.

Apple Fruit Fool

Serves 4

Make exactly as the Luxury Fruit Fool, substituting 450 g
(1 lb) peeled, cored and sliced apples (prepared weight) for
the gooseberries.

Berry Fruit Fool

Serves 4

Make exactly as the Luxury Fruit Fool, substituting 425 ml
(¾ pt) sweetened purée made from fresh raspberries,
strawberries or loganberries. Alternatively, use purée made
from stewed red or black currants or plums.

Economical Fruit Purée

Serves 6 to 8

Make as previously described, substituting 575 ml (1 pt)
freshly made custard for cream.

Batters without Beating

Galettes or Brown Pancakes

Perfect for making those famous Brittany-style galettes or pancakes, wholemeal batter is both unusual and distinctly flavoured. Well worth trying.

Plastic Blade

50 g (2 oz) plain flour, sifted
50 g (2 oz) wholemeal flour
Pinch of salt
2 Grade 3 (standard) eggs
150 ml (¼ pt) cold water
150 ml (¼ pt) cold milk
Melted white cooking fat or lard

Makes 8 to 10

1   Put the flours, salt, eggs, water and milk into processor bowl. Run machine for 5 to 6 counts.

2   Pour batter into a jug. Cover. Refrigerate for a minimum of 1 hour.

3   To make the galettes, lightly brush a 20-cm (8-inch) heavy-based frying pan with melted fat. Heat until hot, pouring off any surplus as this could cause galettes to stick.

4   Pour in just enough batter to cover base of pan very thinly. Cook until underneath is golden; about ¾ minute. Turn. Cook other side until golden. Remove from pan. Keep hot.

5   Repeat, using up rest of batter. Fold each galette in half and half again, arrange in dish and coat with lightly sweetened and heated-through apple purée. Alternatively, in the true French style, spread each galette with jam, then fill with ice-cream and roll up.

6   For savoury galettes, fill with either grated cheese and ham, fried onions or fried tomatoes and mushrooms.

Rich Pancake Batter

Use for pancakes and Yorkshire pudding.

Plastic/Metal Blade

125 g (4 oz) plain flour, sifted
Pinch salt
2 Grade 3 (standard) eggs
275 ml (½ pt) milk (or ½ milk and ½ water)
2 tsp melted butter or margarine (for velvety texture)

Makes 6 to 8

1　Place flour, salt, eggs and milk (or milk and water) into the processor bowl with fat. Run machine for 5 to 6 counts.

2　Pour into a jug. Cover. Refrigerate for 1 hour. Stir before use.

Pancakes

Prepare batter as directed above. To cook pancakes, follow method given for galettes or brown pancakes. Sprinkle with lemon juice and sugar. Roll up. Serve straight away.

Plain Batter

Prepare batter as directed above, using only 1 egg.

Pastry without Tears

Shortcrust Pastry

Metal Blade

225 g (8 oz) plain flour
Pinch of salt
50 g (2 oz) lard or white cooking fat, cubed
50 g (2 oz) block margarine or butter, cubed
2 tbsps cold water

1   Sift flour and salt into processor bowl. Add fats. Run machine for 12 to 15 counts or until mixture looks like fine breadcrumbs. Add water. Run machine for another 2 to 3 counts or until mixture forms itself into a dough which holds together. If necessary, add a little extra water.

2   Turn onto a floured surface. Knead lightly until smooth. Wrap in foil. Refrigerate for at least 30 minutes before using.

Notes

(a)   For sweet pastry, add 3 level tsp caster sugar with the fats.

(b)   If fats are soft, use plastic blade instead of metal.

Fluffy Shortcrust Pastry

Use instead of flaky pastry for sweet and savoury dishes.

Metal Blade

225 g (8 oz) self-raising flour
Pinch of salt
25 g (1 oz) lard or white cooking fat, cubed
75 g (3 oz) block margarine or butter, cubed
2 tbsp cold milk

1   Sift flour into processor bowl. Add salt and fats. Run machine for 10 to 12 counts or until the mixture looks like coarse breadcrumbs.

2   Add milk. Run machine for another 2 to 3 counts or until mixture forms itself into a firm dough which holds together. If necessary, add a little extra milk.

3   Turn onto a lightly floured surface. Knead lightly until smooth. Wrap in foil. Refrigerate for at least 30 minutes before using.

Notes

(a)   For sweet pastry, add 3 level tsp caster sugar with the fats.

(b)   If fats are soft, use plastic blade instead of metal.

Rich Shortcrust Pastry

Metal Blade

225 g (8 oz) plain flour
Pinch of salt
75 g (3 oz) lard or white cooking fat, cubed
50 g (2 oz) block margarine or butter, cubed
1 Grade 3 (standard) egg yolk
1½ tbsp cold water

1   Sift flour and salt into processor bowl. Add fats. Run machine for 12 to 15 counts or until mixture looks like fine breadcrumbs.

2   Add egg yolk and water. Run machine for another 2 to 3 counts or until mixture forms itself into a dough which holds together. If necessary, add a little extra water.

3   Turn onto a floured surface. Knead lightly, until smooth. Wrap in foil. Refrigerate for at least 30 minutes before using.

Notes

(a)   For sweet pastry, add 3 level tsp caster sugar with the fat.

(b)   If fats are soft, use plastic blade instead of metal.

Wholemeal Shortcrust Pastry

A tasty and nourishing pastry for savoury flans, tarts and pies.

Metal Blade

125 g (4 oz) self-raising flour
Pinch salt
125 g (4 oz) wholemeal flour
50 g (2 oz) lard or white cooking fat, cubed
50 g (2 oz) block margarine or butter, cubed
2½ tbsp cold water

1   Sift flour and salt into processor bowl. Add wholemeal flour and fats.

2   Run machine for 12 to 15 counts, or until mixture looks like fine breadcrumbs. Add water. Run machine for another 5 to 6 counts or until mixture forms itself into a firm dough which holds together. If necessary, add a little extra water because brown flour absorbs more liquid than white.

3   Turn out onto a floured surface. Knead lightly until smooth. Wrap in foil. Refrigerate for at least 30 minutes before using.

Cottage Cheese Pastry

A special pastry with origins either in Austria or Hungary — or both! It has a superb flavour and a natural 'puff' when baked. Use for either sweet or savoury dishes.

Plastic/Metal Blade

125 g (4 oz) plain flour, sifted
Pinch salt
125 g (4 oz) well-chilled butter
125 g (4 oz) cottage cheese

1   Put all the ingredients into processor bowl. Run machine for 10 to 14 counts or until the pastry begins to form a ball.

2   Turn onto a floured surface and knead lightly until fairly smooth.

3   Film-wrap and chill for 1 hour in the refrigerator.

Wholemeal Cottage Cheese Pastry

Make as directed above, but use ½ plain white flour and ½ wholemeal.

Cherry Brandy Savarin
Credit – Flour Advisory Bureau

Cheese Scone Round
Credit – Colman's Mustard

A Baker's Dozen — and More

Plain Scones

Feather-light scones which are all-purpose and team congenially with savoury spreads or jams and honey.

Metal Blade

225 g (8 oz) self-raising flour
1 level tsp baking powder
25 g (1 oz) butter or block margarine, cubed
7 tbsp cold milk
Beaten egg or extra milk for brushing over tops

Makes 8

1   Pre-heat oven to 230°C (450°F), Gas 8. Grease thoroughly a flat or shallow baking tray. Dust lightly with flour.

2   Sift flour and baking powder into processor bowl. Add butter or margarine. Run machine for about 8 counts or until mixture resembles fine breadcrumbs.

3   With machine still running, pour milk into processor tube and mix until ingredients form a soft dough which holds together in a ball around the blade.

4   Remove from bowl carefully. Turn onto a well-floured surface. Knead lightly until smooth. Roll out to 1¼ cm (½ inch) in thickness.

5   Cut into 8 rounds with a 6¼-cm (2½-inch) plain or fluted biscuit cutter, gathering up and re-rolling trimmings to give required number of scones.

6   Transfer to the prepared tray. Brush tops with beaten egg or milk. Bake for about 12 to 15 minutes or until well-risen and golden.

7   Remove from oven. Transfer and cool on a wire rack. Break apart when just cold. Butter and serve.

Sweet Scones

Makes 8

Follow recipe for plain scones, adding 25 g (1 oz) caster sugar to processor bowl with sifted flour and baking powder.

Cheese Scones

Makes 8

Follow recipe for plain scones but sift flour and baking powder into processor bowl with 1½ level tsp powder mustard and ½ level tsp salt. Add 50 g (2 oz) diced Cheddar or Edam cheese. Run machine until mixture resembles fine breadcrumbs and cheese is grated; about 10 to 12 counts.

Cheese Scone Round *(see picture facing page 149)*

Makes 8

Make cheese scones as directed. Shape into round 2½ cm (1 inch) in thickness. Transfer to a greased and floured baking tray. Brush with egg. Mark into 8 triangles. Bake for 15 to 20 minutes at 220°C (425°F), Gas 7 or until well-risen and golden. Cool on wire rack. Break apart when cold.

Patricia's Party Cheese Scones

Grating Disc

Plastic Blade

125 g (4 oz) Cheddar cheese, cubed
225 g (8 oz) self-raising flour
½ level tsp baking powder
75 g (3 oz) margarine
½ level tsp salt
¼ level tsp dry mustard
Large pinch white pepper
Cold water
Milk

Makes 10 to 12

1   Using grating disc, feed cheese through processor tube, pressing lightly with plunger. Remove about 1 tbsp of cheese and reserve.

2   Put plastic blade into machine and add flour, baking powder, margarine and seasonings. Run for 7 counts.

3   Add about 4 to 5 tbsp cold water and run again for 2 counts. If necessary add a little more cold water, but do not make dough too moist. Turn onto a floured surface. Knead lightly until smooth.

4   Roll out to about 2½ cm (1 inch) in thickness. Using a 5-cm (2-inch) cutter, stamp into 10 to 12 rounds. Transfer to a greased baking tray.

5   Brush with milk. Sprinkle with remaining grated cheese.

6   Bake for about 15 to 18 minutes at 230°C (450°F), Gas 8 or until scones are well-risen and golden.

7   Lift onto cooling rack. Cool. Split and butter before serving.

Dropped Scones

Akin to a batter, dropped scones are very easy to make and a tea-time treat at any time of year.

Metal or Plastic Blade

125 g (4 oz) self-raising flour
Large pinch of salt
1 level tbsp caster sugar
150 ml (¼ pt) cold milk
15 g (½ oz) melted butter
1 Grade 3 (standard) egg
Melted white cooking fat for frying

Makes about 20

1   Place all ingredients, except melted fat, in processor bowl. Run machine until all ingredients are blended to a smooth batter; about 12 counts.

2   Pour into a jug. Cover. Refrigerate for 1 hour. To cook, brush heavy-based pan with melted fat. Heat until hot but not smoking. Drop in separate tablespoonfuls of batter.

3   Fry until golden underneath and bubbles rise slowly to the top and break; about 2 to 3 minutes. Flip over. Fry until golden.

4   Remove from pan and stack in a folded tea towel to keep warm. Repeat, using up all the batter. Serve while still warm with butter or clotted cream and either maple syrup, jam, honey or golden syrup.

Savoury Dropped Scones

Makes about 20

Follow recipe for dropped scones but omit sugar and include 1 level tsp powder mustard. Serve warm with butter and either cheese, freshly cooked bacon or cold ham.

Corn 'Fritters'

Makes about 20

A simple version of an American favourite, designed as an accompaniment to fried chicken and fried bananas. Follow recipe for dropped scones but omit sugar and include 1 level tsp powder mustard. After pouring batter into jug, stir in 2 heaped tbsp cooked sweetcorn, either canned or frozen. Fry as directed.

155

Brown Sultana Scones

Plastic/Metal Blade

150 g (5 oz) self-raising flour
75 g (3 oz) wholemeal flour
2 rounded tsp baking powder
Pinch salt
50 g (2 oz) margarine
6 to 7 tbsp milk
75 g (3 oz) sultanas

Makes 8 to 9

1   Put flours, baking powder, salt and margarine into processor bowl. Run for 15 to 18 counts.

2   Add most of the milk and run again for 2 counts.

3   Add sultanas. Run machine for a further 2 counts.

4   Turn onto a floured surface. Knead lightly.

5   Roll out to 2½ cm (1 inch) in thickness. Cut into 8 or 9 rounds with a 5-cm (2-inch) cutter.

6   Place on a greased and floured baking tray. Bake for 15 to 18 minutes at 220°C (425°F), Gas 7, by which time scones should be well-risen and golden.

7   Lift onto a cooling rack. Cool. Split. Butter before serving.

Fruit Loaf

Metal Blade

Yeast Liquid
150 ml (¼ pt) boiling water
150 ml (¼ pt) cold water
2 level tsp caster sugar
25 g (1 oz) fresh yeast or 1 level tbsp dried yeast

Dry Ingredients
450 g (1 lb) plain flour
75 g (3 oz) block margarine or butter, cubed
50 g (2 oz) caster sugar
125 g (4 oz) mixed dried fruit

Glaze
Beaten egg

Makes a 1-kg (2-lb) size loaf

1   For yeast liquid, mix together boiling and cold water. Add sugar. Crumble in fresh yeast or stir in dried yeast. Leave in the warm until frothy, allowing up to 15 minutes.

2   Tip dry ingredients (except fruit) into processor bowl. Run machine for about 20 counts or until mixture resembles fine breadcrumbs.

3   Add yeast liquid and run machine for about 15 counts or until dough is formed.

4   Add fruit. Run machine for 3 counts, which should be just long enough to incorporate fruit without chopping it up too much.

5   Turn dough out onto a floured surface. Knead until smooth and no longer sticky. Return to washed and dried bowl which should be lightly greased.

157

6   Cover with a greased plate and leave to rise in a warm place until dough doubles in size. (A sink filled with hot water or the linen cupboard are good places.)

7   Turn risen dough onto a floured surface. Knead lightly until smooth. Shape to fit a 1-kg (2-lb) well-greased loaf tin.

8   Place in tin. Cover with greased greaseproof paper. Leave in a warm place until dough reaches top of tin. Brush with egg. Uncover.

9   Bake for 45 minutes in an oven set to 225°C (425°F), Gas 7. Leave in tin for 5 minutes then turn out onto a wire cooling rack. Leave until completely cold before slicing.

Sticky Cinnamon Bun Cakes *(see picture facing page 164)*

Metal Blade

Yeast Liquid
2 tbsp boiling water
2 tbsp cold water
1 level tsp caster sugar
15 g (½ oz) fresh yeast or 2 level tsp dried yeast

Other Ingredients
225 g (8 oz) plain flour
¼ level tsp salt
75 g (3 oz) butter, melted
1 Grade 3 (standard) egg, beaten
3 tbsp clear honey
3 level tsp cinnamon
50 g (2 oz) walnuts, chopped first in processor
Extra clear honey for glazing

Serves 8

1   For yeast liquid, combine boiling and cold water. Add sugar. Crumble in fresh yeast or stir in dried yeast. Leave in the warm until frothy, allowing up to 15 minutes.

2   Sift flour and salt into processor bowl. Add yeast liquid, butter and egg. Run machine for about 15 counts or until a softish dough forms itself around the blade.

3   Turn out onto a floured surface. Knead lightly until smooth, working in a little extra flour if dough is too wet or extra warm water if too dry.

4   Return to a clean, dry and lightly greased bowl. Cover with a greased plate. Leave in the warm until dough doubles in size; about 1 to 1½ hours in the linen cupboard or a sink of hottish water.

5   Turn onto a floured surface. Knead quickly until smooth. Roll into an oblong measuring 30 by 20 cm (12 by 8 inches).

6   Spread with honey then sprinkle with cinnamon and nuts. Roll up, starting from one of the longer sides. Cut into 8 slices of even thickness.

7   Place slices in greased 20-cm (8-inch) sandwich tin. Cover with greased paper. Leave in the warm until the slices have doubled in size and begin to meet each other. Uncover.

8   Bake for about 35 to 40 minutes in oven pre-heated to 200°C (400°F), Gas 6. Remove from oven and leave for 5 minutes. Turn out onto a wire rack and invert on to a second one so that the top of cake is facing.

9   Brush top with honey while still warm. Break apart when just cold. Eat fresh.

Hot Cross Buns

Metal Blade

Yeast Liquid
2 tbsp boiling water
2 tbsp cold water
2 level tsp caster sugar
25 g (1 oz) fresh yeast or 1 level tbsp dried yeast

Dry Ingredients
450 g (1 lb) plain flour
1 level tsp salt
2 level tsp mixed spice
25 g (1 oz) caster sugar
50 g (2 oz) softened butter or margarine

Other Additions
1 Grade 3 (standard) egg
4 tbsp boiling water   )
4 tbsp cold milk   ) mixed
50 g (2 oz) currants
50 g (2 oz) sultanas

Glaze
2 rounded tbsp granulated sugar
2 tbsp milk
2 tbsp water

Makes 12

1   For yeast liquid, mix together boiling and cold water.
    Add sugar. Crumble in fresh yeast or stir in dried yeast.
    Leave in the warm until frothy, allowing up to 15
    minutes.

2   Tip all dry ingredients into processor bowl. Run
    machine for about 20 counts or until mixture resembles
    fine breadcrumbs.

3   Add frothed up yeast liquid and unbeaten egg with water and milk mixture. Run machine until a dough is formed which gathers together around the blade; about 15 counts.

4   Add currants and sultanas. Run machine for 3 counts, which should be just long enough to incorporate fruit without chopping it up too much.

5   Turn out dough onto a floured surface. Knead until smooth and no longer sticky. Return to a washed and dried bowl which should be lightly greased.

6   Cover with a greased plate and leave to rise in a warm place until dough doubles in size. (A sink filled with hot water or the linen cupboard are good places.)

7   Turn risen dough onto a floured surface. Knead lightly until smooth. Divide into 12 equal-sized pieces. Shape into round buns.

8   Stand on 1 or 2 well-greased baking trays. Cover with greased greaseproof paper. Leave in the warm until buns double in size. Uncover.

9   Cut a cross on each. Bake for 20 to 25 minutes in an oven set to 220°C (425°F), Gas 7. To make glaze, place all ingredients in pan. Heat gently until sugar dissolves. Boil for a few minutes until tacky.

10 Remove buns from oven. Transfer to wire rack. Brush with glaze. Leave until cool before cutting and buttering.

Tips

(a) If preferred, omit milk and use all water.

(b) Instead of cutting a cross on each bun, make crosses on top of each uncooked bun with dampened strips of shortcrust pastry.

(c) To save time, buns may be brushed with golden syrup or honey instead of the glaze. Alternatively, they may be brushed with beaten egg before baking and left unglazed.

Brown Soda Bread

Metal Blade

225 g (8 oz) plain wholewheat flour
¼ level tsp salt
1 level tsp bicarbonate of soda
25 g (1 oz) block margarine, softened
150 ml (¼ pt) sour milk* or fresh milk with 2 tbsp lemon juice added

1 Sift flour, salt and bicarbonate of soda into processor bowl. Add margarine. Run machine for 6 counts.

2 While the processor is running, pour milk through processor tube. Run for a further 12 counts or until dough forms a ball.

3 Turn onto a floured surface and shape into 12½-cm (5-inch) diameter round. Transfer to a greased and floured baking tray. Mark loaf into four even triangles with the back of a knife.

4 Bake for 12 minutes in an oven set to 220°C (425°F), Gas 7. Reduce heat to 180°C (350°F), Gas 4. Bake for a further 10 to 12 minutes or until loaf is well-risen, golden and firm. Cool on a wire rack. Break apart into sections when cold.

*Due to modern processing techniques, sour milk is hard to find outside farms. Therefore city dwellers are advised to use fresh milk and lemon juice.

Cheese Loaf

Looking exactly like a cake, this savoury loaf is a tea-time or high-tea treat if cut into healthy wedges and served plain or buttered with whole tomatoes and chunks of cucumber. It is also nourishing.

Metal Blade

125 g (4 oz) mature Cheddar cheese, cubed
125 g (4 oz) butter or block margarine, softened
225 g (8 oz) self-raising flour
1 rounded tsp baking powder
1 level tsp powdered mustard
½ level tsp salt
2 Grade 3 (standard) eggs
5 tbsp cold milk

Serves 6 to 8

1   Grease thoroughly a ½-kg (1-lb) loaf tin. Line base and sides with greased greaseproof or Bakewell non-stick parchment paper.

2   Place cheese in processor bowl. Run machine for 10 to 12 counts or until finely grated.

3   Add all remaining ingredients. Run machine for 10 counts. Scrape down sides. Run for a further 10 counts.

4   Transfer to the prepared tin. Bake for 1 hour at 190°C (375°F), Gas 5, by which time the loaf should be well-risen and golden.

5   Turn out and cool on wire rack. Store in an airtight tin when cold.

Sticky Cinnamon Bun Cake
Credit – Gale's Honey

Lemon Curd Tarts
Credit – Jif Lemon Juice

Quick as Lightning Cakes and Biscuits

Victoria Sandwich

Metal Blade

125 g (4 oz) self-raising flour
1 level tsp baking powder
125 g (4 oz) caster sugar
125 g (4 oz) soft margarine or softened butter
2 Grade 3 (standard) eggs (at room temperature)
½ tsp vanilla essence (optional)

Serves 6

1   Butter 2 × 17½-cm (7-inch) sandwich tins. Line the bases of the tins with greased, greaseproof paper or Bakewell non-stick parchment paper. Set oven to 180°C (350°F), Gas 4.

2   Sift flour and baking powder into processor bowl. Add all remaining ingredients. Run machine until the contents are well-mixed and smooth; 25 to 30 counts.

3   Divide evenly between the prepared tins. Bake for 25 to 30 minutes or until well-risen and golden. Turn out and cool on wire racks.

4   Before serving, sandwich together with jam. Dust top with sifted icing or caster sugar.

West-Country Sandwich
Serves 6
Sandwich layers together with jam and either clotted or whipped cream.

Lemon Sandwich
Serves 6
Follow recipe for Victoria Sandwich but add 1 level tsp finely grated lemon peel to processor bowl with rest of ingredients. Sandwich together with lemon curd (see page 195) by itself, or with lemon curd and whipped cream.

Feather Sandwich

Serves 6

Follow recipe for Victoria Sandwich but use 75 g (3 oz) self-raising flour and 25 g (1 oz) cornflour.

Almond Sandwich

Serves 6

Follow recipe for Victoria Sandwich but omit vanilla essence. Instead, add ½ tsp almond essence. Sandwich together with raspberry or apricot jam.

Date Cookies

Plastic/Metal Blade

175 g (6 oz) block margarine, softened
75 g (3 oz) light Muscovado sugar
225 g (8 oz) wholemeal flour
125 g (4 oz) stoned cooking dates, coarsely chopped

Makes 24 to 30

1   Put margarine, sugar and wholemeal flour into processor bowl. Run machine for 5 counts or until mixture begins to bind together.

2   Add dates. Run machine for a further 2 counts.

3   Turn mixture onto a floured surface, divide into four and roll each into lengths of 3¾ cm (1½ inches) in diameter. Wrap each length in greaseproof paper. Chill for 1 hour.

4   Cut each roll into 1¼-cm (½-inch) pieces. Place on a greased baking tray. Bake for about 20 to 25 minutes at 160°C (325°F), Gas 3. Cool slightly before lifting onto a wire cooling rack.

Chocolate Sandwich

Reliable and delicious.

Metal Blade

175 g (6 oz) self-raising flour
1 rounded tsp baking powder
25 g (1 oz) cocoa powder
175 g (6 oz) caster sugar
175 g (6 oz) butter, softened
3 Grade 2 (large) eggs
1 tsp vanilla essence
3 tbsp cold milk

Serves 8

1   Sift flour, baking powder and cocoa into processor bowl. Add all remaining ingredients.

2   Run machine for 20 counts. Switch off. Scrape down sides. Run for a further 30 counts.

3   Divide mixture equally between 2 × 20-cm (8-inch) greased and base-lined sandwich tins.

4   Bake for 30 minutes at 180°C (350°F), Gas 4, by which time cakes should be well-risen, firm to the touch and shrink slightly away from the sides of the tin.

5   Turn out onto a wire cooling racks. Peel away paper. Leave cakes until cold. Sandwich together with whipped cream. Dust the top with sifted icing sugar.

Chocolate Layer Cake

This is a variation of the Chocolate Sandwich above, which is layered together with Chocolate Butter Cream (see recipe below).

Chocolate Butter Cream

125 g (4 oz) unsalted butter, softened
225 g (8 oz) icing sugar, sifted
50 g (2 oz) melted and cooled chocolate
2 tsp milk
1 tsp vanilla essence

1   Place all ingredients in processor bowl. Run machine for 20 counts. Switch off. Scrape down sides.

2   Run machine for a further 15 counts. Transfer to bowl. Harden slightly in the refrigerator before using (about 30 to 45 minutes).

Mocha Gateau with Walnuts

Serves 10 to 12

Make up Chocolate Sandwich Cake as directed. Whip until thick 425 ml (¾ pt) double cream together with 3 level tsp caster sugar and 3 to 4 level tsp instant coffee powder (not granules). Slice both layers of cake in half horizontally. Sandwich together with cream. Spread more cream thickly over top and sides. Stud top with walnut halves. Chill for 2 hours in refrigerator before cutting.

Almond Cake

Plastic/Metal Blade

175 g (6 oz) block margarine, softened and cubed
175 g (6 oz) caster sugar
3 Grade 3 (standard) eggs
125 g (4 oz) self-raising flour
1 level tsp baking powder
50 g (2 oz) ground almonds
25 g (1 oz) ground rice
6 drops almond essence

Serves 6

1   Grease thoroughly a 17½-cm (7-inch) round cake tin. Dust with flour.

2   Place all ingredients in processor bowl. Run machine for about 20 counts, or until the mixture is well blended.

3   Spread smoothly into the prepared tin and bake for 1 hour in an oven set to 180°C (350°F), Gas 4. When cake is cooked it should feel firm yet spongy when pressed lightly with the finger.

4   Allow to cool for a few minutes before turning onto a wire cooling rack. Cut when cold. Store leftovers, separately from biscuits, in an airtight tin.

Butter Madeira Cake

An old favourite — to be eaten with a glass of Madeira wine! Now more usual to have at tea-time, Madeira cake should, traditionally, have a couple of strips of citron peel placed on top about halfway through baking time. However, citron peel is not that easy to come by and so this version has been kept plain and unadorned. And it's just as good!

Metal Blade

225 g (8 oz) plain flour
2 level tsp baking powder
175 g (6 oz) caster sugar
175 g (6 oz) butter, softened
3 Grade 2 (large) eggs (kitchen temperature)
2 tbsp cold milk
1 tsp vanilla essence

Makes a 15-cm (6-inch) cake

1   Brush a 15-cm (6-inch) round cake tin or a ½-kg (1-lb) loaf tin with melted butter. Line base and sides with greased greaseproof paper or ungreased Bakewell non-stick parchment paper.

2   Sift flour and baking powder into processor bowl. Add all remaining ingredients. Run machine for 20 counts.

3   Scrape down sides. Run machine for a further 30 counts.

4   Transfer to the prepared tin. Spread top evenly with a knife. Bake in an oven set to 160°C (325°F), Gas 3 for 1½ hours or until a wooden cocktail stick, pushed gently into the centre of the cake, comes out clean with no uncooked pieces of mixture clinging to it.

5   Leave in tin for 15 minutes. Turn out onto a wire cooling rack. Do not remove paper if cake is to be stored. If to be cut and eaten when cold, peel away paper while cake is lukewarm. Store leftovers in an airtight tin separately from biscuits.

Seed Cake

Make exactly as Butter Madeira but add 2 to 3 level tsp caraway seeds after scraping down sides of processor bowl.

Orange Cake

Make exactly as Butter Madeira but omit vanilla. Add 1 level tsp finely grated orange peel instead.

Lemon Cake

Make exactly as Butter Madeira but omit vanilla. Add 1 level tsp finely grated lemon peel instead.

Chocolate Speckle Cake

Make exactly as Butter Madeira but crush 1 large milk flake bar and add to processor bowl after scraping down sides.

Raisin Cake

Make exactly as Butter Madeira but add 75 g (3 oz) seedless raisins to processor bowl after scraping down sides.

Walnut Cake

Make exactly as Butter Madeira but finely chop 75 g (3 oz) walnuts into processor bowl before adding rest of ingredients.

Spicy Cake

Make exactly as Butter Madeira but add 2 to 3 level tsp mixed spice with other ingredients.

173

Chocolate Shells or Whirls

Metal or Plastic Blade

75 g (3 oz) soft margarine
75 g (3 oz) dark brown Muscovado sugar
75 g (3 oz) plain flour
25 g (1 oz) cornflour
25 g (1 oz) cocoa powder
1 Grade 3 (standard) egg

Filling (optional)
Chocolate Butter Cream (page 170)

Makes 12

1   Place margarine and sugar in processor bowl. Run machine for 12 to 15 counts or until both ingredients are well-creamed.

2   Sift together flour, cornflour and cocoa powder. Add to bowl with egg. Work ingredients to a softish paste by running machine for a further 6 to 8 counts.

3   Spoon mixture into an icing bag fitted with 1¼-cm (½-inch) star-shaped pipe. Pipe 12 shells (or 5-cm or 2-inch whirls) onto a greased baking tray.

4   Bake for 12 minutes in an oven set to 190°C (375°F), Gas 5. Leave on the tray for 5 minutes. Remove carefully to a wire cooling rack. Either sandwich together in pairs, when completely cold, with Chocolate Butter Cream or, alternatively, leave plain.

Chocolate Walnut Cookies

Makes 12

By varying the fat in some recipes a very different result can be achieved, and these chocolate walnut cookies are a good example. A variation of the chocolate whirls, I used butter instead of margarine and the biscuits flattened out completely! Also no piping or rolling was required. Make up chocolate shell or whirl mixture, substituting softened (but not melted) butter for the margarine. Roll into 12 balls with damp hands. Flatten with fingers. Press a piece of walnut onto the centre of each. Bake and cool as directed. *Do not* sandwich together.

Cinnamon Chocolate Walnut Cake

A North American import, this has been a favourite cake for many years. It has a wonderful flavour, stays moist for days and, straight from the oven and thickly sliced, happily doubles as a pudding. For a special treat, serve the cake sliced and buttered; the pudding with whipped cream or Brandy Butter (page 103).

Metal Blade

50 g (2 oz) walnuts
350 g (12 oz) self-raising flour
1 rounded tsp cinnamon
1 rounded tbsp cocoa
½ level tsp salt
75 g (3 oz) soft brown sugar, light variety
2 Grade 3 (standard) eggs
50 g (2 oz) butter or margarine, melted
275 ml (½ pt) cold milk
1 tsp vanilla essence

Serves 8 to 10

1   Place walnuts in processor bowl. Chop coarsely; about 6 counts.

2   Sift together flour, cinnamon, cocoa and salt. Add to processor bowl with all remaining ingredients. Run machine for 6 counts or until the contents are well mixed.

3   Spread smoothly in a 1-kg (2-lb) loaf tin, well-greased and lined with greased greaseproof paper or ungreased Bakewell non-stick parchment paper.

4   Bake for 1¼ hours in an oven set to 180°C (350°F), Gas 4, by which time the cake should be well-risen and golden. To test, push a wooden cocktail stick gently into centre. If it comes out clean with no uncooked pieces of mixture clinging to it, then the cake is cooked.

5   Remove from oven and turn out onto a wire cooling rack. Leave until cold before removing paper.

Orange Brazil Nut Cake

Follow recipe and method for Cinnamon Chocolate Walnut Cake, but substitute brazil nuts for walnuts and chop coarsely. Omit cinnamon and cocoa but include 2 level tsp finely grated orange peel, which should be added with 75 g (3 oz) caster instead of brown sugar. Reduce milk by 1 tbsp.

Walnut Coffee Rum Cake

A glamorous confection for a very special tea, or to serve to friends with evening coffee.

Metal Blade

50 g (2 oz) walnuts
3 Grade 3 (standard) eggs
3 level tsp instant coffee powder)
1 level tsp baking powder   )   sifted
175 g (6 oz) self-raising flour   )
175 g (6 oz) butter, softened
175 g (6 oz) soft brown sugar
1 tbsp cold milk
4 tbsp dark rum

Filling and Topping
275 ml (½ pt) double cream
50 g (2 oz) caster sugar
2 tbsp raspberry jam

Serves 10

1   Place walnuts in processor tube. Chop fairly finely; 20 counts.

2   Place all remaining ingredients in processor bowl. Run machine until the contents are well blended, allowing 15 to 18 counts. Stir round to make sure walnuts are completely incorporated.

3   Divide between 2 × 20-cm (8-inch) sandwich tins, well-greased and their bases lined with greased greaseproof paper or Bakewell non-stick parchment paper.

4   Bake for 25 to 30 minutes in an oven set to 180°C (350°F), Gas 4 or until cakes are well-risen and just beginning to pull away from the sides of the tins. Remove from oven.

5   Turn out onto a wire cooling rack. Peel away paper. Pour 2 tbsp rum over the base of each cake and leave it to soak in.

6   When cakes are completely cold, whip cream and sugar together until thick. Beat in jam. Slice each cake in half. Sandwich layers together with the cream and jam mixture.

7   Spread the remainder of the cream and jam over the top of the cake. Transfer to a serving dish. Chill for 1 hour in the refrigerator before cutting.

Spicy Fruit Cake

A full-flavoured, family cake that everybody's mother makes and bakes!

Metal Blade

225 g (8 oz) self-raising flour
125 g (4 oz) butter, softened
125 g (4 oz) caster sugar
1 level tsp mixed spice
1 rounded tsp baking powder
2 Grade 3 (standard) eggs
1 tsp vanilla essence
2 tbsp cold milk
125 g (4 oz) mixed dried fruit

Makes 8 portions

1   Butter thoroughly a 15-cm (6-inch) round cake tin or 450-g (1-lb) oblong loaf tin. Line base and sides with greaseproof or Bakewell non-stick parchment paper. If using greaseproof, brush with more melted butter.

2   For cake, place all ingredients except fruit into processor bowl. Run machine until the contents are well mixed; 12 to 15 counts.

3   Add fruit. Run machine for 3 to 4 counts. Stir mixture round with spatula. Spread smoothly into the prepared tin. Bake for 1½ hours in oven set to 180°C (350°F), Gas 4.

4   The cake is cooked when well-risen and golden, and when a metal skewer or cocktail stick, pushed gently into centre, comes out clean with no uncooked pieces of mixture sticking to it.

5   Leave in tin for 10 minutes. Turn out onto a wire cooling rack. Peel away paper. Cut when cold. Store leftovers in an airtight tin.

Variations

Farmhouse Cake

Reduce dried fruit to 75 g (3 oz). Add also 25 g (1 oz) coarsely chopped glacé cherries and 25 g (1 oz) lightly toasted almonds.

Date and Lemon Cake

Start off by breaking up 125 g (4 oz) block cooking dates into chunky pieces. Place in processor bowl fitted with metal blade. Run machine until the dates are coarsely chopped; 2 to 3 counts. Add cake ingredients as given, *excluding* other dried fruit, but including finely grated peel of 1 small lemon. Run machine for 12 counts or until ingredients are well mixed.

Walnut and Sultana

Substitute 125 g (4 oz) sultanas for mixed fried fruit. Add 25 g (1 oz) broken walnuts with rest of cake ingredients.

Coconut Cake

Omit fruit and spice. Substitute 50 g (2 oz) desiccated coconut. Increase milk by 1 tbsp.

Seed Cake

Omit fruit and spice. Substitute 1 level tbsp caraway seeds. If liked, add 1 level tsp finely grated lemon peel.

Rich Fruit Cake

A very easy, satisfying, family-size cake.

Plastic/Metal Blade

175 g (6 oz) plain flour
1 level tsp baking powder
1 level tsp mixed spice
125 g (4 oz) block margarine, softened and cubed
125 g (4 oz) Muscovado brown sugar
2 Grade 3 (standard) eggs
2 tbsp cold milk
350 g (12 oz) mixed dried fruit
50 g (2 oz) chopped mixed peel

1   Grease thoroughly a 17½-cm (7-inch) cake tin. Line with greased greaseproof paper.

2   Sift together flour, baking powder and spice. Put into processor bowl with margarine, sugar, eggs and milk. Run for 10 to 15 counts or until ingredients are well mixed.

3   Add fruit and peel. Run machine for 2 counts. Stir ingredients well to mix.

4   Spoon some of mixture into the prepared tin. Remove blade. Scrape out remaining mixture and add to tin. Spread smoothly with a knife.

5   Bake at 160°C (325°F), Gas 3 for about 1½ hours, or until a wooden cocktail stick, pushed gently into the centre of the cake, comes out clean.

6   Leave in the tin for about 15 minutes before turning out onto a wire cooling rack.

Cream Cheese Cake

A wickedly rich cheese cake, adaptable enough to serve for coffee mornings, afternoon tea or as a dinner-party sweet.

Metal Blade

125 g (4 oz) digestive biscuits
675 g (1½ lb) curd cheese or sieved cottage cheese
    (the former is preferable)
175 g (6 oz) caster sugar
2 level tbsp cornflour
3 Grade 3 (standard) eggs
142 ml (¼ pt) double cream
1 tsp vanilla essence
Finely grated peel and juice of 1 small lemon

Serves 10

1   Butter thoroughly a 20-cm (8-inch) spring pan form with clip-on sides. Set oven to 150°C (300°F), Gas 3.

2   Break up biscuits. Place in processor bowl. Crush finely, allowing about 10 to 15 counts.

3   Spread over base of the prepared tin. Wash and dry processor bowl. Replace metal blade.

4   Place all remaining ingredients in processor bowl. Run machine for 20 counts. Stir thoroughly. Run machine for a further 15 counts or until the mixture is very smooth.

5   Pour into tin over crumbs. Bake for 1¼ hours. Switch off heat. Open oven door. Leave cake to cool in oven for 30 minutes.

6   Take out of oven and cool completely before unclipping sides. Serve on the cake tin base.

Cream-Topped Cheese Cake

After cake has cooked for its 1¼ hours, remove from oven and cover top with 142 ml (5 oz) soured cream. Return to oven for 30 minutes. Continue as directed in point 5.

Novelty Cheese Cakes

Cover crumb layer with either 225 g (8 oz) sliced strawberries or raspberries, 350 g (12 oz) stoned cherries, or 1 medium can well-drained peach slices *before* topping with cheese mixture.

Traditional Shortbread

A beautiful short shortbread, ideally suited to any festive occasion.

Metal Blade

175 g (6 oz) plain flour
125 g (4 oz) butter, softened
50 to 75 g (2 to 3 oz) caster sugar
1 extra level tsp caster sugar for top

Makes 8 wedges

1   Place all ingredients, except extra sugar, in processor bowl. Run machine until a soft, paste-like dough is formed; about 26 to 30 counts.

2   Spread smoothly into 17½-cm (7-inch) round sandwich tin. Prick all over lightly then ridge edges with a fork for a decorative effect.

3   Sprinkle with extra sugar. Bake for 1 hour in an oven set to 150°C (300°F), Gas 3, by which time shortbread should be a very pale straw colour.

4   Remove from oven. Leave in the tin until almost cold. Cut into 8 wedges. Cool completely on a wire rack. Store in an airtight tin.

Hazelnut Shortbread

Grind 50 g (2 oz) hazelnuts in processor bowl fitted with metal blade. Leave in bowl. Add ingredients as given in Traditional Shortbread. Follow same method. Sprinkle with extra sugar. Bake as directed. Cool. Cut into wedges. Cool.

Note
As the Shortbread mixture has a high butter content, greasing of the tin in either of these recipes is unnecessary.

French Biscuits

Metal/Plastic Blade

175 g (6 oz) soft margarine
175 g (6 oz) plain flour
50 g (2 oz) icing sugar, sifted
¼ tsp almond or vanilla essence
10 walnuts, broken into pieces

Makes 28 to 30

1   Put all ingredients, except walnuts, into processor bowl. Run machine for 8 to 10 counts.

2   Turn mixture onto a well-floured surface. Divide into four and roll into lengths of 2½-cm (1-inch) diameter. Wrap each length in floured greaseproof paper or foil. Chill for 1 hour as mixture is *very* soft.

3   With a floured knife, cut the rolls into pieces just over 1¼ cm (½ inch) in thickness. Place them on an ungreased baking tray, leaving room between each because they spread. Flatten them slightly with a floured knife and place a piece of walnut on the centre of each.

4   Bake at 180°C (350°F), Gas 4 for about 30 minutes or until pale gold.

5   Allow the biscuits to cool slightly before lifting them onto a wire cooling rack. Store in an airtight tin when cold.

Shortbread Cookies
Makes 36 to 40
By using butter the whole character of the French Biscuits can be changed completely, which means you use one basic recipe for two entirely different biscuits. For the Cookies, substitute softened butter for margarine. Continue as directed for French Biscuits. Bake for about 20 minutes only because butter causes biscuits to brown more rapidly than margarine.

Cheese Biscuits

Shredding Disc

Plastic/Metal Blade

150 g (5 oz) mature Cheddar cheese, cubed
175 g (6 oz) self-raising flour   )
¼ level tsp baking powder   )   sifted
125 g (4 oz) block margarine, cubed
½ level tsp salt
Large pinch of cayenne pepper and white pepper
1 Grade 3 (standard) egg

Makes about 60

1   Using shredding disc, feed cheese through processor tube, pressing well down with plunger. Remove disc and take out about 25 g (1 oz) of grated cheese for sprinkling over top of biscuits (optional).

2   Change to plastic/metal blade. Add flour, baking powder, margarine and seasonings to processor bowl. Run machine for 10 counts.

3   Add most of egg to processor bowl. Run machine again for about 5 counts or until the mixture forms itself into large crumbs.

4   Turn onto a floured surface and knead mixture lightly together. Divide in two and film wrap. Chill for 30 minutes.

5   Roll each piece of pastry out fairly thinly. Cut into rounds of between 3¾ and 5 cm (1¾ to 2 inches) in diameter. Transfer to a lightly greased baking tray. Mix remaining egg with a little water. Brush over tops of biscuits. If liked, sprinkle with a little extra grated cheese. Bake for about 10 to 12 minutes (or until golden brown) in an oven set to 200°C (400°F), Gas 6. Cool on a wire rack.

Flips and Shakes and other Drinks

Cool Yogurt Lime

A tinglingly refreshing drink for hot summer days.

Metal/Plastic Blade

Place 225 g (8 oz) natural yogurt in processor bowl with 1 tbsp lime cordial and 275 ml (½ pt) chilled lemonade. Run machine for 10 counts. Pour into 2 tumblers. Add 2 or 3 ice cubes to each.
Serves 2

Mandarine Hothouse Tea

Fragrant with a distinctive tang of orange blossom.

Metal Blade

Place 8 ice cubes in processor bowl. Run machine for 20 to 22 counts or until the cubes are crushed. Divide between 2 tumblers. Half fill with cold, strained tea. Add 2 tbsp mandarine liqueur to each. Top up the tumblers with chilled soda water until they are two-thirds full. Stir. Serve straight away.
Serves 2

Coffee Milk Frappé

The best for coffee addicts.

Metal Blade

Place 8 ice cubes in processor bowl. Run machine for 10 counts. Add 2 rounded tsp instant coffee powder and the same of caster sugar. Run machine for a further 10 counts. Pour in 275 ml (½ pt) chilled milk. Run machine for 5 counts. Pour into 2 glasses. Drink straight away while ice is in crystals.
Serves 2

Banana Milk Shake

Metal Blade

Cut 1 large banana into chunks. Add 1 heaped tbsp vanilla ice cream and 2 level tsp caster sugar. Run machine for 6 to 8 counts. With machine still running, pour 275 ml (½ pt) chilled milk gradually down the processor tube. Transfer to 2 glasses. Sprinkle lightly with powdered cinnamon and drink straight away.
Makes 2 average glasses

Dutch Nog

Metal/Plastic Blade

Pour 2 tbsp ginger wine, 4 tbsp Advocaat and 275 ml (½ pt) tonic water into processor bowl. Run machine for 10 counts or until the mixture is frothy. Pour into 2 glasses. Add 3 ice cubes to each. Drink straight away.
Serves 2

Chutneys, Relishes and Marmalades

Lemon Curd *(see picture facing page 165)*

Whizzed together in the processor and then cooked gently until thick, this is a handsomely flavoured spread which should be stored in the refrigerator. It is not quite as thick as shop-bought varieties.

Metal/Plastic Blade

6 tbsp bottled lemon juice
1 level tsp finely grated lemon peel
3 Grade 3 (standard) eggs
125 g (4 oz) butter (unsalted for preference), melted
225 g (8 oz) caster sugar

Makes about 350 g (12 oz)

1   Place all ingredients in processor bowl. Run machine for 10 counts.

2   Pour into a saucepan. Cook long and slowly, stirring continuously, until curd just reaches boiling point and thickens sufficiently to cling to the spoon.

3   Remove from heat. Cool. Spoon into a clean, dry jar. When it is cold cover as for jam.

Dark Thick Marmalade

Slicing Disc

1 kg (2 lb) bitter oranges
1 medium sweet orange
2 medium lemons
2¼ litres (4 pts) water
2 kg (4 lb) soft brown sugar (dark variety)
1 level tbsp black treacle

Makes about 3 kg (6 lb)

1   Wash fruit thoroughly and wipe dry. Cut off any printed lettering on skin.

2   Cut each fruit in half. Squeeze out juice. Reserve. Remove pips. Tie in a clean piece of thin cloth.

3   Cut fruit 'shells' into quarters. Feed through processor tube, pressing well down with plunger.

4   Place fruit 'shells', juice and water into a preserving pan or large, heavy saucepan. Bring to boil. Lower heat. Cover. Simmer for 1 hour. Uncover. Continue to simmer further for 1 hour or until the quantity is reduced by about half. Stir from time to time.

5   Add pips and sugar. Cook, stirring over gentle heat, until sugar dissolves. Bring to boil. Boil fairly briskly, uncovered, for about 30 minutes or until setting point* is reached.

6   Stir in treacle. Cook for a further 2 minutes. Remove from heat. Take out bag of pips. Leave marmalade until lukewarm before potting and covering. Use clean, dry jars.

*To test for setting, pour a little marmalade onto a cold saucer. If, after 2 minutes, a skin forms on top which crinkles when touched, setting point has been reached. The temperature on a sugar thermometer should reach 140°C or 220°F.

Zippy Nut Relish

Fresh and lively, this speciality relish is appetisingly different when eaten with meat, poultry and offal dishes.

Metal Blade

1 large orange, peeled and segmented
125 g (4 oz) fresh cranberries
50 g (2 oz) brazil nuts
50 g (2 oz) onion
¼ level tsp salt

Serves 6

1   Place all ingredients in processor bowl. Run machine for about 15 counts or until ingredients are coarsely chopped.

2   Transfer to a dish. Serve straight away. Store leftovers for up to 3 days in a covered container in the refrigerator.

Grapefruit Marmalade

Slicing Disc

2 grapefruit   )
1 sweet orange   )   total 1 kg or 2 lb
2 lemons   )
2¼ litres (4 pts) water
Granulated sugar (quantity in Method, Point 5)
1 level tsp citric acid (available from chemists)
1 rounded tsp butter

Makes about 2 kg (4 lb)

1   Wash fruit thoroughly and wipe dry. Cut off any printed lettering on skin.

2   Halve all the fruit and remove pips. Tie pips in a clean piece of thin cloth. Leave on one side for the time being. Squeeze juice out of fruit.

3   Feed all the fruit 'shells' through processor tube, pressing down lightly with plunger. Empty fruit directly into a preserving pan or large saucepan.

4   Add juice and water. Bring to boil. Lower heat. Cover. Simmer for 1 hour. Uncover. Continue to simmer for a further 45 minutes to 1 hour or until the quantity has been reduced by half.

5   Measure fruit pulp in a measuring cup and allow 450 g (1 lb) granulated sugar to every 575 ml (1 pt) pulp. Put both into a pan, together with the citric acid and the bag of pips.

6   Cook, stirring over gentle heat, until sugar dissolves. Bring to boil. Boil fairly briskly, uncovered, for about 30 minutes or until setting point is reached. (For details, see Dark Thick Marmalade on pages 196-7.) Stir often to prevent sticking.

7   Take off heat. Leave until lukewarm before potting and covering. Use clean, dry jars.

Red Red Relish

Metal Blade

225 g (8 oz) onions, peeled and quartered
1 medium red pepper, de-seeded and cut into strips
2 garlic cloves, peeled
1½ kg (3 lb) unpeeled tomatoes, quartered
2 medium cooked beetroots, skinned and cubed
125 g (4 oz) soft brown sugar (dark variety)
1 level tsp powder mustard
1 tsp Worcester sauce
275 ml (½ pt) red wine vinegar
2 level tbsp tomato purée
2 level tsp salt

Makes about 2 kg (4 lb)

1   Place onions, pepper and garlic in processor bowl. Run machine until the contents are fairly finely chopped; 10 to 12 counts.

2   Add tomatoes and beetroot. Run machine for a further 5 to 7 counts or until the contents are coarsely chopped. Tip all ingredients into a mixing bowl. Sprinkle with sugar, mustard and Worcester sauce.

3   Toss. Beat together vinegar, purée and salt. Add to vegetables. Stir round. Ladle into clean, dry jars.

4   Cover as for jam. Refrigerate for up to 3 weeks. Serve with cold meats, hardboiled eggs and cheese.

Rhubarb Chutney

Metal Blade

450 g (1 lb) rhubarb, trimmed of leaves
450 g (1 lb) onions, peeled and quartered
150 ml (¼ pt) water
275 ml (½ pt) malt vinegar
450 g (1 lb) soft brown sugar
½ level tsp pepper
2 level tsp salt
1 level tsp *each*, mixed spice and cinnamon
¼ level tsp mustard seeds
6 cloves
Juice of 1 medium lemon

Makes about 1½ kg (3 lb)

1   Wash rhubarb and cut into 2½-cm (1-inch) lengths.

2   Place onions in processor bowl, in several batches, and run machine until they are finely chopped; about 6 to 8 counts.

3   Put onions and water into saucepan. Bring to boil. Lower heat. Cover. Simmer until onions are tender; about 20 minutes.

4   Add all remaining ingredients except lemon. Bring to boil. Simmer, uncovered, until mixture is soft and thick; about 40 minutes. Stir often to prevent stickings.

5   Add lemon juice to taste. Cook for a further 2 minutes.

6   Remove from heat. Allow to cool before spooning into clean, dry jars. Cover as you would for jam.

Acknowledgements

The authors wish to thank the manufacturers of the following
machines and ingredients used in the testing of the recipes in
this book.
Bowater Scott Corporation Ltd.
Edward Billington (Sugar) Ltd.
Braun Multiquick
Brittany Fruit and Vegetables
Buxted Chickens
Carmel Produce
Colman's
Corning Ltd (Pyrex Glassware)
Hostess Toasters
Kenwood Food Processors, models A530 and A531
Kraft Foods Ltd.
Magimix Food Processor
Moulinex Maxima Food Processor
Mushroom Growers Association
Pifco Food Processor
Precision Engineering Co. (Reading) Ltd.,
          (Waymaster Scales)
The Prestige Group Ltd.
RHM Foods Ltd.
Ring Electric
Robot Chef Food Processor
Rowenta Food Processor
Sarsons' Vinegars
Sharwood's
South African Avocados
Sunbeam Food Processor
Toshiba Food Processor
Tupperware Company
Wheelbarrow Dutch Butter

INDEX

Almond:
  Cake 171
  Sandwich 168
American-Style Coleslaw 77
Appetising Meat Plait 50
Apple(s):
  Fruit Fool 134
  Pie, Deep Southern 126-7
  Sauce 91
  in Waldorf Salad 84
Aubergine(s):
  in Ratatouille 73
  Soup, Spiced 25
Avocado(s):
  Cream Soup,
    Mexican-Style 26
  and Egg Pâté 5
  and Gammon Grill 45
  in Mexican Guacamole 8
  Salad Cream 101
  Soup, Chilled 17
Bacon:
  with Brussel Sprouts 59
  in Party Ham and Chicken
    Risotto 47
  Potted 46
Baked Coffee Pudding 125
Baked Haddock Portions 32
Bakewell Tart:
  with Lemon Curd 129
  Patricia's 128
  Traditional 129
Banana:
  Milk Shake 192
  Spice Pudding 121
Basic White Coating
  Sauce (1) 89
Basic White Coating
  Sauce (2) 89
Batter:
  Plain Pancake 139
  Rich Pancake 139
Batter Dishes:
  Devilled Kidney
    Pancakes 55
  Galettes, or Brown
    Pancakes 137-8
  Pear and Honey
    Pancakes 127
Bean and Horseradish Dip 118

Beef:
  in Appetising Meat Plait 50
  and Beetroot, One Pot 48
  in Meat 'Pie' Express 51
  in Sesame Pepper Mince
    Cakes 49
Beetroot:
  Jellied Consommé 18
  One-Pot Beef and 48
Berry Fruit Fool 134
Biscuits:
  Cheese 187
  Date Cookies 168
  French 186
  Hazelnut Shortbread 185
  Shortbread Cookies 186
  Traditional Shortbread 185
Braised Leeks 64
Brandy:
  Butter Sauce 103
  Sauce 90
Brazil (Nut):
  Cake, Orange 177
  Slivers Savoury 107
  and Peanut Stuffing 108
Bread:
  Brown Soda 163
  Sauce 92
Brown Pancakes 137-8
Brown Soda Bread 163
Brown Sultana Scones 156
Brussel Sprouts with
  Bacon 59
Buns:
  Hot Cross 161-2
  Sticky Cinnamon Bun
    Cakes 159-60
Butter Madeira
  Cake 172-3
Cabbage:
  in American-Style
    Coleslaw 77
Cake(s):
  Almond Sandwich 168
  Butter Madeira 172-3
  Chocolate Layer 170
  Chocolate Sandwich 169
  Chocolate Shells or
    Whirls 174
  Chocolate Speckle 173

Chocolate Walnut Cookies 175
Cinnamon Chocolate
    Walnut 176-7
Coconut 181
Cream Cheese 183
Cream-Topped Cheese 184
Date and Lemon 181
Farmhouse 181
Feather Sandwich 168
Fruit Cake, Rich 182
Fruit Cake, Spicy 180
Lemon 173
Lemon Sandwich 167
Mocha Gateau with
    Walnuts 170
Novelty Cheese 184
Orange 173
Orange Brazil Nut 177
Raisin 173
Rich Fruit 182
Seed 173, 181
Spicy 173
Spicy Fruit 180
Victoria Sandwich 167
Walnut 173
Walnut Coffee Rum 178-9
Walnut and Sultana 181
West-Country Sandwich 167
Caper Sauce 90
Carrot(s):
    and Courgette Soup,
        Ian's 22
    Ginger-Glazed 60
    and Potato Soup 23
Cauliflower:
    in Chilled Dubarry Cream
        Soup 16
    Marinaded 79
    'Slaw' 78
Celery:
    with Juniper Berries 61
    and Tomato Soup,
        On-the-Spot 28
    in Waldorf Salad 84
Cheese:
    Biscuits 187
    Dip, Cheddar 116
    Loaf 164
    Potatoes, English-Style 70
    Sauce 93
    Scone Round 152
    Scones 152
    Scones, Patricia's Party 153
Cheese, Cottage:

Pastry 147
Pastry, Wholemeal 147
and Pepper Dip,
    Chivey 117
Cheese Cake(s):
    Cream 183
    Cream-Topped 184
    Novelty 184
Cherry Brandy:
    Savarin 130-1
    Syrup 130-1
Chicken:
    Creole 35
    en Papillote 41
    Flan, Monday 38
    Liver Pâté, Extremely
        Rich 7-8
    Risotto, Party Ham and 47
Chicory, Cucumber and
    Tomato Salad 81
Chilled Dubarry Cream
    Soup 16
Chivey Cottage Cheese and
    Pepper Dip 117
Chocolate:
    Butter Cream 170
    Layer Cake 170
    in Mocha Gateau with
        Walnuts 170
    Sandwich 169
    Sauce 90
    Shells or Whirls 174
    Speckle Cake 173
    Walnut Cake,
        Cinnamon 176-7
    Walnut Cookies 175
Chutney, Rhubarb 200
Cinnamon:
    Chocolate Walnut
        Cake 176-7
    Bun Cakes, Sticky 159-60
Cocktail Sauce 97
Coconut Cake 181
Cod:
    in Patricia's Speciality
        Fish Pie 36-7
    in 'Stuffed' Fish Cutlets in
        White Wine 33
    Provençale 34
Coffee:
    Milk Frappé 191
    Pudding, Baked 125
    Rum Cake, Walnut 178-9
    Sauce 90

204

Sponge Pudding, Steamed 124
Coleslaw, American-Style 77
Coleslaw with Pineapple 77
Consommé, Jellied
    Beetroot 18
Cool Yogurt Lime 191
Corn 'Fritters' 155
Cottage Cheese:
    Pastry 147
    Pastry, Wholemeal 147
    and Pepper Dip, Chivey 117
Courgette(s):
    and Carrot Soup, Ian's 22
    Fried 63
    'Quick Braise' 62
    in Ratatouille 73
Cream Cheese Cake 183
Cream-Topped Cheese
    Cake 184
Cream, Chocolate Butter 170
Creamed Mushrooms 11
Creamy French Dressing 98
Creole Chicken 35
Cucumber:
    Salad, Middle-Europe 83
    and Tomato Salad,
        Chicory 81
    and Yogurt Mousse 82
Curd, Lemon 195
Dark, Thick Marmalade 196-7
Date:
    Cookies 168
    and Lemon Cake 181
Deep Southern Apple
    Pie 126-7
Devilled Kidney Pancakes 55
Dips:
    Bean and Horseradish 118
    Cheddar Cheese 116
    Chivey Cottage Cheese and
        Pepper 117
    Spicy Mayonnaise 117
    Taramosalata 115
    Walnut and Garlic 111
Dressings:
    Creamy French 98
    French 99
    Green Pepper 99
    Hardboiled Egg 100
    Horseradish 100
    Thousand Island 98
Dropped Scones: 154
    Savoury 155
Dutch Nog 192

Egg:
    and Avocado Pâté 5
    Dressing, Hardboiled 100
    Mayonnaise, Whole 96
English-Style Cheese
    Potatoes 70
Farmhouse Cake 181
Feather Sandwich 168
Fish Dishes:
    Baked Haddock Portions 32
    Kipper Pâté 4
    Old English Kedgeree 37
    Patricia's Speciality Fish
        Pie 36-7
    Provençale Cod 34
    Smoked Mackerel Pâté 3
    'Stuffed' Fish Cutlets in
        White Wine 33
    Stuffed Mackerel 31
    Taramosalata 115
    Tuna Mousse 9
Five-Minute Mushroom and
    Tomato Soup 27
Flan, Monday Chicken 38
Frappé, Coffee Milk 191
French Biscuits 186
French Dressing: 99
    Creamy 98
Fried Courgettes 63
'Fritters', Corn 155
Fruit Cake:
    Spicy 173
    Rich 182
Fruit Fool:
    Apple 134
    Berry 134
    Luxury 133
    Rhubarb 133
Fruit Loaf 157-8
Fruit Purée, Economical 134
Galettes 137-8
Gammon Grill,
    Avocado and 45
Garlic:
    Dip, Walnut and 111
    Mayonnaise 97
Ginger-Glazed Carrots 60
Golden Onion Soup 15
Grapefruit Marmalade 198-9
Gratin Dauphinoise 70
Green Mayonnaise 97
Guards' Pudding 123
Haddock:
    in Old English Kedgeree 37

205

in Patricia's Speciality
Fish Pie 36-7
Portions, Baked 32
in 'Stuffed' Fish Cutlets in
White Wine 33
Ham and Chicken Risotto,
Party 47
Hardboiled Egg Dressing 100
Hazelnut:
Potato Scallop 71
Shortbread 185
Honey Pancakes,
Pear and 127
Horseradish:
Dip, Bean and 118
Dressing 100
Hot Cross Buns 161-2
Ian's Carrot and Courgette
Soup 22
Instant Mint Sauce 93
Juniper Berries, Celery and 61
Kedgeree, Old English 37
Kidney Pancakes, Devilled 55
Kipper Pâté 4
Lamb:
Chops en Papillote 41
Marinaded Stuffed 39
Patties, Minted 42
Shoulder,
Vegetable-Stuffed 40
Leeks, Braised 64
Lemon:
Cake 173
Cake, Date and 181
Curd 195
Sandwich 167
Lettuce Soup 21
Lime, Cool Yogurt 191
Liver Pâté:
Country 6
Extremely Rich Chicken 7-8
Loaf:
Cheese 164
Fruit 157-8
Veal and Prune 52
Low-Calorie Mushroom
Spaghetti Sauce 94
Luxury Fruit Fool 133
Mackerel:
Pâté, Smoked 3
Stuffed 31
Madeira Cake, Butter 172-3
Mandarine Hothouse Tea 191
Marinaded Cauliflower 79

Marinaded Stuffed Lamb 39
Marmalade:
Dark Thick 196-7
Grapefruit 198-9
Marsala Pizza Squares 10-11
Marzipan, Walnut 112
Mayonnaise:
in Avocado Salad
Cream 101
in Cocktail Sauce 97
Dip, Spicy 117
Garlic 97
Green 97
in Hardboiled Egg
Dressing 100
in Tartare Sauce 97-8
in Thousand Island
Dressing 82
Tuna 98
Whole Egg (main recipe) 96
Meat Dishes:
Appetising Meat Plait 50
Avocado and Gammon Grill 45
Devilled Kidney Pancakes 55
Marinaded Stuffed Lamb 39
Meat 'Pie' Express 51
Minted Lamb Patties 42
Monday Chicken Flan 38
One-Pot Beef and Beetroot 48
Party Ham and Chicken
Risotto 47
Pork Cutlets in Beer 44
Potted Bacon 46
Sausage Meat Crumble Slices 54
Sesame Pepper Mince Cakes 49
Stuffed Pork Shoulder 43
Terrine of Veal 53
Veal and Prune Loaf 52
Vegetable-Stuffed Lamb
Shoulder 40
Meat 'Pie' Express 51
Mexican Guacamole 8
Mexican-Style Avocado Cream
Soup 26
Middle-Europe Cucumber Salad 83
Milk Shake, Banana 192
Minted Lamb Patties 42
Mint Sauce, Instant 93
Mixed Nut Burgers 110
Mocha Gateau with Walnuts 170
Monday Chicken Flan 38
Mousse:
Cucumber and Yogurt 82
Strawberry 132

206

Tuna 9
Mushroom(s):
  Creamed 11
  Dressed 85
  with Onion, Stir-Fry 65
  Sauce 90
  Spaghetti Sauce, Low-Calorie 94
  and Tomato Soup, Five-Minute 27
Mustard Sauce 90
New Year's Eve Soup 19-20
Nog, Dutch 192
Nut Dishes:
  Brazil and Peanut Stuffing 108
  Mixed Nut Burgers 110
  Savoury Brazil Nut Slivers 107
  Savoury Nut Crumble Topping 109
  Savoury Nut Stuffing 109
  Walnut and Garlic Dip 111
  Walnut Marzipan 112
  Zippy Nut Relish 197
Nut Relish, Zippy 197
Old Colonial Tomato Soup 24
Old English Kedgeree 37
One-Pot Beef and Beetroot 48
Onion:
  Sauce 94
  Soup, Golden 15
On-the-Spot Celery and Tomato
    Soup 28
Orange:
  Brazil Nut Cake 177
  Cake 173
Pancake(s):
  Batter, Plain 139
  Batter, Rich 139
  Brown, or Galettes 137-8
  Devilled Kidney 55
  Pear and Honey 127
Pan Potatoes 72
Parsley Sauce 90
Parsnip(s):
  à la Crème 66
  Sauté 67
Party Ham and Chicken Risotto 47
Pastry:
  Cottage Cheese 147
  Fluffy Shortcrust 144
  Rich Shortcrust 145
  Shortcrust 143
  Wholemeal Cottage Cheese 147
  Wholemeal Shortcrust 146
Pâté:
  Country Liver 6
  Egg and Avocado 5

Extremely Rich Chicken Liver 7-8
Kipper 4
Smoked Mackerel 3
Terrine of Veal 53
Patricia's:
  Bakewell Tart 128
  Party Cheese Scones 153
  Speciality Fish Pie 36-7
Peanut Stuffing, Brazil and 108
Pear and Honey Pancakes 127
Pease Pudding 68
Pepper (Green):
  Dip, Chivey Cottage
    Cheese and 117
  Dressing 99
  in Ratatouille 73
  Salad, Tomato and 80
Pie:
  Deep Southern Apple 126-7
  Patricia's Speciality Fish 36-7
Pineapple Sauce 104
Pizza Squares, Marsala 10-11
Potted Bacon 46
Pork:
  Shoulder, Stuffed 43
  Cutlets in Beer 44
Potato(es):
  and Carrot Soup 23
  English-Style Cheese 70
  in Gratin Dauphinoise 70
  Pan 72
  Savoyard 69
  Scallop, Hazelnut 71
  Snow 70
Poultry Dishes:
  Brazil and Peanut Stuffing
    (for chicken and turkey) 108
  Chicken en Papilotte 41
  Creole Chicken 35
  Extremely Rich Chicken
    Liver Pâté 7-8
  Monday Chicken Flan 38
  Party Ham and Chicken
    Risotto 47
  Savoury Nut Crumble Topping
    (for poultry casseroles) 109
  Savoury Nut Stuffing
    (for chicken and turkey) 109
Pouring Sauce 89
Provençale Cod 34
Puddings:
  Baked Autumn Pudding 122
  Baked Coffee Pudding 125
  Banana Spice Pudding 121

207

Bakewell Tart with
   Lemon Curd 129
Cherry Brandy Savarin 130-1
Deep Southern Apple Pie 126-7
Economical Fruit Purée 134
Guards' Pudding 123
Luxury Fruit Fool
   (and variations) 133
Patricia's Bakewell Tart 128
Pear and Honey Pancakes 127
Pease Pudding 68
Steamed Coffee Sponge
   Pudding 124
Strawberry Mousse 132
Traditional Bakewell Tart 129
'Quick Braise' Courgettes 62
Raisin Cake 173
Ratatouille 73
Relish:
   Red, Red 199
   Zippy Nut 197
Rhubarb:
   Chutney 200
   Fruit Fool 133
Rich Fruit Cake 182
Risotto, Party Ham and Chicken 47
Rum:
   Butter Sauce 103
   Cake, Walnut Coffee 178-9
   Sauce 90
Salads:
   American-Style Coleslaw 77
   Cauliflower 'Slaw' 78
   Chicory, Cucumber and
      Tomato 81
   Cucumber and Yogurt Mousse 82
   Dressed Mushrooms 85
   Marinaded Cauliflower 79
   Middle-Europe Cucumber
      Salad 83
   Pineapple Coleslaw 77
   Tomato and Pepper 80
   Waldorf 84
Sandwich:
   Almond 168
   Chocolate 169
   Feather 168
   Lemon 167
   Victoria 167
   West-Country 167
Sauces:
   Apple 91
   Basic White Coating Sauce (1) 89
   Basic White Coating Sauce (2) 89

Brandy 90
Brandy Butter 103
Bread 92
Caper 90
Cheese 93
Chocolate 90
Coffee 90
Instant Mint 93
Low-Calorie Mushroom
   Spaghetti 94
Mushroom 90
Mustard 90
Onion 94
Parsley 90
Pineapple 104
Pouring 89
Rum 90
Sweet 89
Tartare 97-8
Tomato 95
Watercress Cream Topping 102
Sausage Meat Crumble Slices 54
Savoury Brazil Nut Slivers 107
Savoury Nut Crumble Topping 109
Scones:
   Brown Sultana 156
   Cheese 152
   Dropped 154
   Patricia's Party Cheese 153
   Plain 151
   Round, Cheese 152
   Savoury Dropped 155
   Sweet 152
Seed Cake 173, 181
Sesame Pepper Mince Cakes 49
Shortbread:
   Cookies 186
   Hazelnut 185
   Traditional 185
Shortcrust Pastry: 143
   Fluffy 144
   Rich 145
   Wholemeal 146
Snow Potatoes 70
Soda Bread, Brown 163
Soups, Cold:
   Chilled Avocado 17
   Chilled Dubarry Cream 16
   Chilled Watercress 20
   Jellied Beetroot Consommé 18
Soups, Hot:
   Five-Minute Mushroom and
      Tomato 27
   Golden Onion 15

208

Ian's Carrot and Courgette 22
Lettuce 21
Mexican-Style Avocado Cream 26
New Year's Eve 19-20
Old Colonial Tomato 24
On-the-Spot Celery and Tomato 28
Potato and Carrot 23
Spiced Aubergine 25
Spiced Aubergine Soup 25
Spicy Cake 173
Spicy Fruit Cake 180
Spicy Mayonnaise Dip 117
Steamed Coffee Sponge Pudding 124
Sticky Cinnamon Bun Cakes 159-60
Stir-Fry Mushrooms with Onion 65
Strawberry Mousse 132
'Stuffed' Fish Cutlets in
    White Wine 33
Stuffed, Lamb Shoulder,
    Vegetable 40
Stuffed Mackerel 31
Stuffed Pork Shoulder 43
Stuffing:
  Brazil and Peanut 108
  Savoury Nut 109
Sweet Sauce 89
Taramosalata 115
Tartare Sauce 97-8
Tea, Mandarine Hothouse 191
Terrine of Veal 53
Thousand Island Dressing 98
Tomato(es):
  and Pepper Salad 80
  in Ratatouille 73
  Salad, Chicory, Cucumber and 81
  Sauce 95
  Soup, Five-Minute
    Mushroom and 27
  Soup, Old Colonial 24
  Soup, On-the Spot Celery and 28
Tuna:
  Mayonnaise 98
  Mousse 9
Veal:
  and Prune Loaf 52
  Terrine of 53
Vegetable Dishes:
  Braised Leeks 64
  Brussel Sprouts with Bacon 59
  Celery with Juniper Berries 61
  English-Style Cheese Potatoes 70
  Fried Courgettes 63
  Ginger-Glazed Carrots 60
  Gratin Dauphinoise 70

Hazelnut Potato Scallop 71
Pan Potatoes 72
  Parsnips à la Crème 66
  Parsnips Sauté 67
  Pease Pudding 68
  Potatoes Savoyard 69
  'Quick Braise' Courgettes 62
  Ratatouille 73
  Snow Potatoes 70
  Stir-Fry Mushrooms with Onion 65
Vegetable-Stuffed Lamb Shoulder 40
Victoria Sandwich 167
Walnut(s):
  Cake 173
  Cake, Cinnamon Chocolate 176-7
  Coffee Rum Cake 178-9
  Cookies, Chocolate 175
  and Garlic Dip 111
  Marzipan 112
  and Sultana Cake 181
  in Waldorf Salad 84
Watercress:
  Cream Topping 102
  Soup, Chilled 20
West-Country Sandwich 167
White Coating Sauce (1), Basic 89
White Coating Sauce (2), Basic 89
Whole Egg Mayonnaise 96
Yogurt:
  Lime, Cool 191
  Mousse, Cucumber and 82